*The keep, Gleaston Castle*

# THE CASTLES
# AND TOWER HOUSES
# OF CUMBRIA

## Mike Salter

FOLLY PUBLICATIONS

# ACKNOWLEDGEMENTS

The photographs in this book were taken by the author between 1979 and 1998. He also prepared the map and the plans. Most of the plans are on scales of 1:400 and 1:800, although there are some site plans at 1:2000. Old postcards and prints are reproduced from originals in the author's collection. Thanks to Marjorie Salter who checked the text, and to Max Barfield, Chris and Frances Bowers, Mike Jackson, and Peter Ryder for help with accommodation, transport and information during field trips.

## AUTHOR'S NOTES

This series of books (see full list inside the back cover) is intended as portable field guides giving as much information and illustrative material as possible in volumes of modest size, weight and price. Quite a lot of information is given on lesser known buildings. The aim has been to mention, where the information is known to the author, owners or custodians of buildings who erected or altered parts of them, and those who were the first or last of a line to hold an estate, an important office, or a title. Those in occupation at the time of historic events such as sieges are also sometimes named. Other owners and occupants whose lives had little effect on the buildings are generally not mentioned, nor are ghost stories, myths or legends.

The books are intended to be used in conjunction with the Ordnance Survey 1:50,000 scale maps. Grid references are given in the gazetteers together with a coding system indicating which buildings can be visited or easily seen by the public from adjacent public open spaces which is explained on page 104. A few grid references for buildings which have left no remains are only approximate.

The books in this series commonly use the pre-1974 county names and boundaries. Cumbria is an exception in that the modern boundaries make more sense than the old ones, so the area covered by this book includes all of the former counties of Cumberland and Westmorland, the Furness district of Lancashire and a small portion of the West Riding of Yorkshire around Sedbergh.

Some of the sites are known by alternative names or different spellings of the same name. Those chosen are generally the ones most commonly in use this century.

Each level of a building is called a storey in this book, the basement being the first storey with its floor near courtyard level unless specifically mentioned as otherwise.

Measurements given in the text and scales on the plans are metric. Although the buildings were designed using feet and inches the metric scales are much easier and were used for all fieldwork. For those who feel a need to make a conversion 3 metres is almost 10 feet. Unless specifically mentioned all dimensions are external at or near ground level, but above the plinth if there is one. On the plans the original work is shown black, post-1800 work is stippled and intermediate periods are hatched.

## ABOUT THE AUTHOR

Mike Salter is 45 and has been a professional writer and publisher since he went on the Government Enterprise Allowance Scheme for unemployed people in 1988. He is particularly interested in the planning and layout of medieval buildings and has a huge collection of plans of churches and castles he has measured during tours (mostly by bicycle and motorcycle) throughout all parts of the British Isles since 1968. Wolverhampton born and bred, Mike now lives in an old cottage beside the Malvern Hills. His other interests include walking, railways, board games, morris dancing, playing percussion instruments and calling dances with a folk group.

Folly Publications, Folly Cottage, 151 West Malvern Rd, Malvern, Worcs, WR14 4AY.
Printed by Severnside Printers, Bridge House, Upton-upon-Severn, Worcs, WR8 0HG.

*Clargyll Hall, a mansion incorporating two bastles.*

## CONTENTS

# INTRODUCTION

There is no certain evidence that Cumbria contained any privately owned defensible residences of the type known to the Normans as castles before 1092. In that year William the Conqueror's son and successor William Rufus invaded Cumbria and took it from the Scots. The district was settled by barons from the south, estates being granted in return for specified periods of military service. The barons in turn gave units of land called manors to their knights, again in return for military service, this system being known as feudalism. This thin veneer of land-owning Normans consolidated their fragile hold on the land by constructing castles as residences, strongholds and status symbols. During William Rufus's campaign castles were built by him or his followers at Carlisle, Bewcastle, Brough and Liddel. Others at Beaumont, Burgh-by-Sands and Maryport may also date from the 1090s.

Bewcastle and Brough lie within the circuits of Roman fortifications and the latter seems to have had stone walls from the start. This, however, was unusual and until the 1150s castles in Cumbria, as elsewhere in England, were mostly of earth and wood. These were quicker, easier and cheaper materials to work with, skilled masons being in short supply compared with carpenters and labourers. A common form comprised an earth mound or motte surmounted by a timber tower with a small palisaded court around it. At the base was a larger court or bailey surrounded by a rampart, palisade and ditch, and containing a hall, chapel, workshops, and stores. The tower on the mound formed a private dwelling for the lord and a last refuge should the weaker bailey defences succumb to an attack. The basic design varied according to the terrain and the labour and time available. A small enclosure with high banks (known to castle experts as a ringwork) was sometimes provided instead of a mound, whilst baileys were omitted or duplicated and made whatever shape and size local circumstances dictated. Natural landscape features were used whenever possible, almost all the early Norman earthworks in Cumbria being carved out of the ends of spurs. There is evidence of the existence of about thirty earthworks of these types in Cumbria dating from the 1090s to the 1190s. Mottes could take more time and effort to construct and the campaign castles needed in a hurry tended to be ringworks, many of which were developed as stone-built castles later on. At Aldingham there is evidence of a ringwork later being heightened into a motte and at Liddel a motte seems to have been added on one side of an already existing ringwork.

0      25

metres

*Castlehaugh, Sedburgh*

*Ringwork at Pennington*

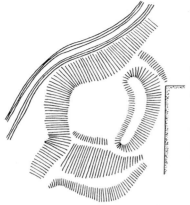

*Plan of Pennington Ringwork*

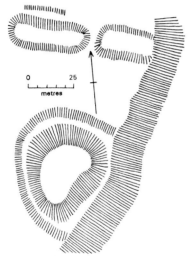

*Plan of Aldingham Motte*

*The keep, Brough Castle*

In 1136 King Stephen was forced to cede Cumbria back to David I of Scotland. David had been brought up in England and had English lands and titles and the Norman lords then ruling Cumbria were generally allowed to remain as long as they acknowledged his overlordship. When Henry II came to the English throne in 1154 he was in a strong position whilst Malcolm, the new Scottish king, was weak. As a result Cumbria passed back to the English Crown in 1157. Afterwards the castles were gradually rebuilt in stone, espcially after the rebellion of 1173-4 when some of them were destroyed.

Unfortunately no certain dates are known for castle construction in Cumbria during the 12th and 13th centuries so buildings there have to be dated by analogy with others elsewhere that can be dated more precisely. Although it could be earlier, the keep at Carlisle may date from the 1150s or 60s. The keep at Appleby is probably of c1170 and the keeps at Brougham and Brough are of c1175-85, the latter replacing a smaller tower of the 1090s or the early 12th century. All these keeps as originally built were square or rectangular towers with the entrance (reached through a forebuilding at Carlisle and Brougham) at the level of the second out of three storeys. This room would be a hall, that below being a storage space, and the top storey being a private chamber for the lord. Appleby and Brough retain two-light windows on the upper storeys, otherwise the windows were small round headed loops. The upper storeys had fireplaces and in the corners were latrines and spiral staircases. All of them have seen a fair amount of alteration over the years. Originally the walls would rise up high above the roof but later on this space was often used

Brough already possessed stone curtain walls, whilst the curtains of both the inner and outer wards at Appleby and Carlisle are of late 12th century origin but with much alteration and repair. Part of an early but short-lived curtain was revealed by excavation at Burgh-by-Sands. At Egremont there is a length of early or mid 12th century curtain walling and a square gatehouse. This castle had a different type of keep in which a shell wall was erected around a small court on the summit of the motte. As the motte here was largely natural it could have borne the weight of this shell not long after the castle was founded. None of the Cumbrian castles have any domestic buildings earlier than the block of c1200 at Brougham so the halls, chambers and workshops of these castles must have still been structures of wood.

The 13th century was a peaceful period for Cumbria and there is surprisingly little work of note from this period in the castles. Egremont has a hall block of some size and distinction (although very ruined) plus about half the circuit of the curtain wall and the lower parts of other domestic buildings. Brough has remains of a mid 13th century gatehouse. At Brougham the curtain walls are 13th century with one rectangular corner tower and an inner gatehouse of the 1290s. Round towers are the norm elsewhere in England in the 13th century but in the North rectangular towers were preferred at all periods, especially in the 14th century. The idea of using towers to provide flanking fire does not seem to have been taken very seriously in the north of England. Loops designed for the discharge of crossbows and longbows are rare in Cumbria, nor are there medieval openings for firearms. In Cumbria there is not a single castle courtyard which is properly flanked all round by towers or turrets. The few round towers that existed in Cumbria have either been destroyed or mostly rebuilt later as at Brough and Cockermouth. There is evidence that Cockermouth was quite a large castle in the 13th century with more than one round tower but as it stands most of it is late 14th century. Appleby had two round towers added to help flank the walls of the outer ward. The smaller of the two has been removed and the other is somewhat altered. At Kendal there is a tower which is a full round (most round towers are actually D-shaped i.e. only round towards the field) straddling the curtain. It is quite crudely built, as indeed is the whole castle, which has a curtain wall around a circular court with a much altered and damaged keep of uncertain date and one other tower which is square. Also possibly of this period is the small walled court originally without any towers or projections at Bewcastle, whilst excavations at Burgh-by-Sands revealed footings of a hall house with a round corner tower.

*Bewcastle Castle*

The Scots never really forgave the English for Edward I's attempt for rule Scotland by installing the puppet king John Balliol in 1292, and then from 1296 onwards trying to rule their kingdom directly himself. During Edward's reign only Scotland suffered from the conflicts but after his death in 1307 both official raids led by or ordered by the Scottish kings and unofficial raids by Scottish borderers acting on their own account were frequent until the union of the Crowns in 1603, although things quietened a little in the 15th century. Consequently the 14th century was a boom period for the erection of defensive structures in Cumbria. Contributions of this period to older castles include hall blocks at Brough, Brougham and Kendal. At Brougham there are other ranges as well, one including a chapel, and c1300 the keep was heightened by one storey with a fine oriel tucked in one corner. Cockermouth was almost entirely rebuilt between 1370 and 1400 with an outer court with a square corner tower and a gatehouse with a barbican and an inner court with another gatehouse and a complete suite of domestic buildings, including a fine tower containing a huge kitchen. Carlisle has two 14th century gatehouses, plus slight remains of another tower, also once a gatehouse. Of new castles of this period Piel is the largest with inner and outer courts with square flanking towers and a magnificent palatial keep with large upper windows in chambers either side of a central corridor reached through a porch with two portcullises. Gleaston has a single court of some size which was probably never finished, although at least two of the corner towers were. At another corner lies a keep long enough to contain a central hall with chambers at each end. Unfortunately it is now very ruined. Kirkoswald, also very ruined, is a much smaller castle with a hall and solar tower filling one side of a court with two towers on the opposite side and a gatehouse on another. A ceiling taken from the solar tower here to Naworth is very fine.

*Irton Hall in 1788*

*Brougham Castle*                    *Millom Castle*

*The palatial keep at Piel Castle*

The erection of fortifications was to some degree controlled by the Crown which granted licences for the embattling of secular buildings. Over a dozen such licences exist for 14th century castles and towers in Cumbria and these help to date the buildings concerned. Each licence has a paragraph relating why permission was being granted (usually this repeats word for word whatever reason the applicant gave), and in Cumbria the reason given was usually the damage caused by recent Scottish raids. The first batch are Dacre, Drumburgh, and Scaleby licensed in 1307, before the raids began in earnest, and Pendragon in 1309. The next batch are Millom and Naworth of 1335, Rose 1336, Triermain 1340, Highhead 1342, Greystoke and Hartley 1353, and Rose again 1355. Finally there are Workington of 1380, and Penrith of 1397 and 1399. Dacre and Pendragon are tower houses or keeps standing alone within moated platforms. The others had courts of modest size with a square or rectangular tower forming a self contained residence for the lord. These towers have an entrance at ground level lead into a vaulted cellar, then a living room above, with a private chamber on top. At Naworth the original iron gate or yett at the entrance still survives. Naworth and Greystoke both seem to have had at least two towers originally. Rose eventually had several towers, a fine suite of domestic buildings, and an outer ward surrounding the inner court. Of other towers for which no licence exists several are of note. Dalton still stands alone, now in a much altered state, especially inside. Sizergh, one of the largest towers of this type, has a wing near the middle of one side and a turret to contain the stair projecting from the opposite side. Arnside also has a wing, set at one end of a long side, making an L-plan. A latrine turret projects at the diagonally opposite corner. The main blocks of both these towers were subdivided on each storey. Muncaster has a square tower house which originally projected from one corner of a rectangular court.

Projections set diagonally are a characteristic of 14th century castles in Cumbria, and indeed the north of England generally. At Greystoke one of the two towers was sited this way in relation to its former court. The keeps at Pendragon and Piel have turrets or buttresses set diagonally, and they also appear on the solar tower at Kirkoswald, the outer gatehouse at Brougham, on the curtain wall at Penrith, and at two diagonally opposite corners of the tower at Dacre. At the last larger square-set turrets seem to have replaced diagonal projections at the other two corners.

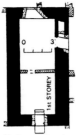

*Skelsmergh: plan*                    *Workington Hall*

Cumbria has several 14th century manor houses where the lord's private room or solar was contained in an impressive tower demonstrating the wealth and power of the builder. Some of these towers could have withstood a sudden but short-lived attack by a small party of raiders. A common plan is a hall with cross-wings containing upper chambers over service rooms at either end. Either or both of the cross-wings could be of three storeys and embattled. Some of them, as at Askham, were large and impressive. Howgill also has this H-shaped plan but was altogether more of a fortress since the cross-wings were large, massively walled, and difficult to enter. This building is often referred to as a castle whilst the others are known as halls. Burnside has remains of a massively walled court on one side and at Beetham and Middleton hall blocks with thinly walled cross-wings lie within walled courts capable of defence. At Yanwath, Hazelslack and Clifton are solar towers, the adjoining halls having vanished at the last two places. The upper parts of the tower at Yanwath and all of the thinly walled tower at Clifton are early 16th century.

Not many entirely new castles and towers were built in Cumbria during the 15th century, although there were several alterations and additions to older buildings. There is a substantial tower at Armathwaite and Hayton had a hall block with a solar tower at one end and a smaller tower at the other end, all later absorbed into a mansion. Askerton has a block with small towers added at each end. A hall block with towers at each end, all much altered, remains at Appleby. At Scaleby there is a hall block of this period. At Penrith two phases of 15th century building saw the erection of four ranges of apartments within the newly built outer walls, plus the addition of another square tower and an adjoining gatehouse.

*Randalholm Hall*                    *Harbybrow Tower*

In the medieval period castle walls were sometimes limewashed outside making them look very different from the way they do today. However dressed stones around windows and doorways would not have been so covered, nor ashlar work. Domestic rooms would have had whitewashed rooms decorated with murals of biblical, historical or heroic scenes mostly painted in red, yellow and black. Wall hangings gradually became more common from the 14th century onwards. Although used in churches, glass was expensive and was uncommon in secular buildings before the 15th century so windows were originally closed with wooden shutters, resulting in the rooms being dark when the weather was too cold or wet for them to be opened. Large openings in the outer walls sometimes had iron bars or projecting grilles even if they were high above ground level, although no medieval examples of this survive. Living rooms usually had fireplaces although some halls had central hearths with the smoke escaping through louvres in the roof. Latrines are common and indicate which rooms were for living, working or sleeping in, rather than just storage space.

Furnishings were sparse in the 13th and 14th centuries although the embrasures of upper storey windows sometimes have built-in stone seats. Great lords owning several castles or manor houses tended to circulate around them, administering their manorial courts and consuming agricultural produce on the spot. Tower houses and solar towers tended to be built by smaller landowners only having one seat and so were more likely to be permanently occupied by a family, but the castles of the greater lords could sometimes be left almost empty when they were not in residence. Servants travelled with the lords and sometimes also portable furnishings such as rugs, wall hangings, cooking vessels and bedding, all kept in wooden chests. The lord and his immediate family and any honoured guests would enjoy a fair degree of privacy, having their own rooms. Servants and retainers enjoyed less comfort and privacy, sharing of beds and communal sleeping in halls and warm places of work like the kitchens and stables being common.

*Naworth Castle*

*Isel Hall*                                    *Blencow Hall*

Cumbria was too remote for its castles to play a part in the dynastic struggles of the 15th century, by the end of which the idea of privately owned fortfications had become outmoded throughout much of England. Developments in cannon had made even the strongest castles vulnerable to a siege by a king or major lord (only kings could usually afford to maintain and transport siege trains). However Cumbria was still subject to Scottish raids and so most lordly dwellings still needed to be secure against fierce but usually short-lived attacks by bands of marauders. Buildings of the 16th century tend to have thinner walls, say 1.2m to 1.5m thick as opposed to over 2m or more before. Naworth has three ranges and a corner tower of the early 16th century. Many of the 14th century towers such as Sizergh now adjoin non-defensive domestic blocks of the 16th and 17th centuries. Bewcastle has a gatehouse and barbican either of the 1470s or the 16th century. Parts of the palace of the Bishops of Carlisle at Rose are early 16th century, whilst Scaleby has a block of the 1590s. Of tower house type buildings of the 16th century, Brackenhill and Kirkandrews have a Scottish look about them and remain inhabited, Drumburgh is a long, much altered building, more a stronghouse than a tower, Ulpha is a much ruined block with a stair wing at the back making a T-plan, and Shank was destroyed in the 1950s. The bastle houses built by tenant farmers from c1590 onwards are described on pages 101-103.

Tower houses in Cumbria have mostly remained in occupation up to the present day, about forty still forming parts of dwellings. Many of them have consequently been much altered and extended, Howgill being an example of a particularly dramatic transformation. Dalton is still roofed but not occupied. The houses with castellated cross-wings have had a mixed fate. Most still have farmers living on site but in each case part of the main building or its outbuildings or courtyard walls are ruinous. The castles mostly had absentee lords during the 16th century and there were periods when the Percy and Dacre estates were held by the Crown and their castles decayed. The many surveys existing for this period mostly show the castles greatly in need of repair. Even strategically important fortresses like Carlisle were poorly maintained. The Civil War finished off most of the proper castles, as only Carlisle escaped either being damaged during a siege, slighted after one, or neglected to the point where parts of the walls fell down. In the 1650s the Lady Anne Clifford patched up the castles of Appleby, Brough, Brougham and Pendragon, but her successors lived down south and after her death in 1676 only Appleby was kept habitable. Carlisle remained in use as a barracks until becoming an ancient monument in the 20th century. The surviving parts of Rose Castle were rebuilt after the Civil War and again in the 19th century. At Cockermouth only the outer gatehouse remains habitable but later ranges within the outer court form a dwelling and offices. Domestic buildings at Scaleby also remain in use, although the tower house and curtain wall are ruinous.

# GAZETTEER OF CASTLES AND TOWERS

## ALDINGHAM MOTTE    SD 278698

On the edge of a cliff above Morecambe Bay is a scrub-covered motte rising 9m high above a ditch 3m deep and 6m wide. The motte measures 31m across on top and was probably created by Michael le Fleming c1100 by filling in an earlier ringwork probably raised by Roger de Poitou, whose possesions were confiscated in 1102. The Flemings still further heightened the motte later in the 12th century but abandoned it in the early 13th century, probably transferring to a nearby moated site. There are slight traces of a ditch 6m wide around a crescentic-shaped bailey to the north.

## APPLEBY CASTLE    NY 685199    O

Ranulph le Meschin founded this castle before 1121 when it passed to the Crown on his succession to his cousin's earldom of Chester. In 1136 King Stephen ceded the castle to the Scots. They held it until Henry II regained control of Cumbria in 1157. He granted Appleby to Hugh de Morville who is assumed to have built the keep immediately before the castle was confiscated for his part in the rebellion of 1173 by the king's sons. Gospatric was fined by Henry II for surrendering the castle too easily to the Scots in 1174. It was granted in 1179 to Theobald de Valoines but reverted to the Crown in 1190. In 1203 King John granted the the castle to Robert de Vipont, nephew of Hugh de Morville, who had died the previous year. Appleby passed by marriage to Roger de Clifford in 1269 who probably added the two round towers.

Thomas, 3rd Lord Clifford, an ardent Lancastrian, remodelled the domestic buildings in the 1450s. After Thomas was killed at the battle of Towton in 1461 Edward IV confiscated the castle and it was not returned until after Richard III's death at Bosworth in 1485. The buiding may have been damaged by the Yorkists and it is uncertain how much it was used subsequently. Leland c1539 describes it as ruinous although it still housed the county gaol. During the Catholic rising in the north of 1569 Henry Clifford, 2nd Earl of Cumberland, had the castle slighted "so as to be of no use to anyone should it be taken". The building was further damaged during the Civil War but in 1651 its restoration as a residence was begun by Anne Clifford, Dowager Countess of Pembroke. With her death in 1676 the four hundred year Clifford association with Appleby ended and the castle passed by marriage to Thomas Tufton, Earl of Thanet. In 1686-8 he took materials from the castles of Brough and Brougham for the construction of a new range of apartments at Appleby. His descendants sold the castle c1950 and it was sold again quite recently.

*Round Tower at Appleby*

The castle consisted of an inner ward with a maximum diameter of 53m and an outer ward 42m wide extending 80m eastwards towards a steep drop to the River Eden. The deep surrounding ditch is crossed only by a causeway on the north. To the NW is a rectangular outer enclosure now containing a square late 17th century stable block, and there are outer enclosures to the south and SW. The inner ward represents a ringwork with its rampart flattened. The keep stands isolated in the middle of it. The inner ward curtain is about 2m thick and dates from the second half of the 12th century. There are no projections apart from buttresses of much later date. One short section adjoining a modern building on the NE is 15th century and the whole of the southern half of the circuit was rebuilt by the Lady Anne Clifford in the 1650s. She evidently saw no need to rebuild the wall dividing the two wards and there is now no sign of a wall or ditch there.

The keep of c1170 is 14.2m square over walls 1.8m thick with clasping corner buttresses rising up 24m as corner turrets with lanterns probably added in 1784. The keep has three storeys, all of them now divided by a crosswall of the 1650s containing fireplaces for the second and third storeys. These two levels have latrines in the NE corner and a pair of original windows with two rectangular lights under a round outer arch in each wall, except that the entrance replaces one window on the second storey. From this level stairs in both the southern corners lead up, an indication that the third storey may have originally been subdivided. Only the SE stair leads down to the basement which had two narrow loops in each of the north and south walls plus one more and what appears to be another ancient entrance in the east wall.

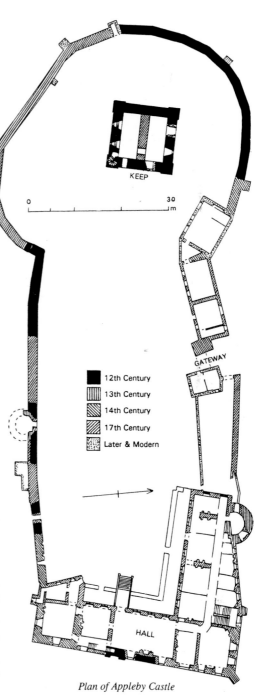

KEEP

0                    30
                     m

12th Century
13th Century
14th Century
17th Century
Later & Modern

GATEWAY

HALL

*Plan of Appleby Castle*

The keep, Appleby

Appleby: interior of keep

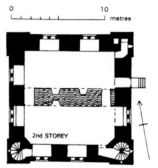

Keep Plan, Appleby

The south curtain wall of the outer ward is late 12th century but much of it has been much rebuilt, a section near the east end being 15th century and a breach west of the site of a 13th century tower about 6.6m in diameter in the middle being closed up again in the 1650s. The doorway further east is also of that date. The north side has suffered even more rebuilding. A portion of the west side of a 15th century gateway tower is the only medieval work between the keep and a 13th century D-shaped tower 8.4m in diameter now adjoining the domestic buildings. West of this gateway tower is a laundry block of the 1650s. The apartments overlooking the drop to the river on the east incorporate a 12th century postern in the middle. The ends of the range were once late 14th century towers about 10m square, rebuilt in the 1450s. That to the north has a buttress on the NE corner, and that to the south has a latrine projection at the SW corner. This tower has work of the 1650s west of it but otherwise the apartments are now mostly of the 1680s with later alterations. A hall 13.5m long by 7.6m wide lies in the middle of the east range with one chamber each end between it and the former towers, that on the north being a chapel. A new range of the 1680s extends 26m west from the back of the chapel and contains a central corridor with five private rooms on the south and several smaller rooms and a scale-and-platt staircase squeezed into an awkwardly shaped space on the north.

## ARMATHWAITE CASTLE    NY 505459

The four storey tower by the west bank of the River Eden is first mentioned in the early 16th century but may have been built by John Skelton after he was granted an estate here by Henry VI in 1444. It appears that a building 16m long by 8m wide over walls up to 1.6m thick was later doubled in width by adding a parallel block to the west. It was sold to the Sandersons in 1712, and then in 1741 passed by marriage to the Milburnes. They remodelled the west front to show a typical Georgian facade of two storeys of living rooms over a service basement with an attic on top. The doorway is broadly rusticated with a straight entablature which is repeated on the basement windows. In 1846 the house was sold to the Earl of Lonsdale, from whom it was acquired by the Ackroyds. They sold the house to the Armstrongs and it was converted into flats but it has now reverted to being a single private dwelling.

## ARNSIDE TOWER    SD 458769    V

This late 14th century building was accidentally burnt in 1602 but repaired and occupied until the roof timbers were removed to Beetham and Knowsley in the 1680s. It has a main block 14.9m long by 10.3m wide over walls 1.2m thick. Each of the four unvaulted storeys was divided into a square main NW room from which was reached a smaller rectangular SE room. The main rooms were connected by a spiral stair rising from the southern jamb of the entrance doorway on the NE. This opens into a kitchen with a fireplace with an oven opening from it within the base of a wing 5m wide projecting 4m from the north of the NE side. Above this wing contains four levels of small rooms. On the upper storeys the SE rooms were bedchambers with fireplaces in the SE wall, latrines in a turret at the south end of that wall, and windows on each of three sides. The crosswall is mostly destroyed and the SW wall and west corner collapsed during a gale in 1884. See front cover photo.

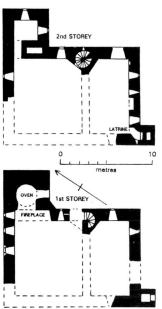

*Plans of Arnside Tower*                    *Armathwaite Castle*

## ASKERTON CASTLE     NY 551692     V

The SE range measures 18.3m by 8m over walls 1.3m thick and is thought to date in part from the 14th century. In c1500-25 Thomas, Lord Dacre, Warden of the West March, added the Dovecot Tower at the north end and the Dacre Tower at the south end, his initials appearing on the outer corner of the latter. Neither tower is as wide as the older block and the re-entrant angles are corbelled across with latrine shutes. He also added a SW range containing a new hall 15.2m long by 7.3m wide, and a still larger NW wing containing barrack accommodation over stables. Part of a stair remains which gave access to the former battlements of the hall range. The castle was forfeited and partly dismantled as a result of the Dacres' involvement with the northern rebellion of 1569. Between 1576 and 1578 the place was occupied by Thomas Carleton but allowed to still further decay. John Musgrave repaired the castle after being granted it in 1598 and shortly afterwards it was described as "a house of good strength and defence, and the only house in Gilsland fit for the Land Sergeant (the Warden's officer) to dwell in". Not long afterwards the Dacre estates passed by marriage to the Howards, although they had to pay Queen Elizabeth a large sum before being allowed to take possession of the castles of Askerton and Naworth. Much remodelling and repair took place in the late 19th century when the SW and NW ranges were mostly rebuilt except for their outer walls, a new wall was built to close off the NE end of the court, and new windows and doorways were provided in the SE range after the floor levels were altered. Further restoration took place in 1922 and the building is still occupied by a tenant as a farmhouse.

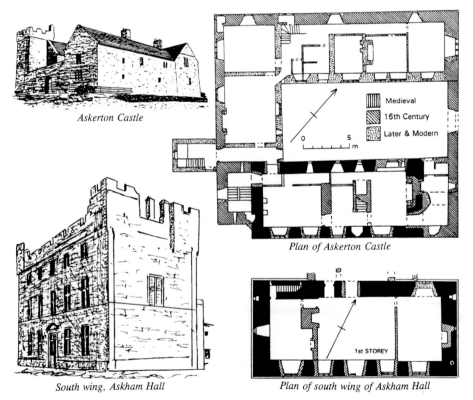

*Askerton Castle*

Medieval
16th Century
Later & Modern

0    5
m

*Plan of Askerton Castle*

*South wing, Askham Hall*

1st STOREY

*Plan of south wing of Askham Hall*

*Askerton Castle*

## ASKHAM HALL   NY 516239

In 1325 Robert de Swynburn's seat here was burnt by the Scots. The manor previously belonged to the de Hellbeck family. The Sandfords are assumed to have built the present house soon after they obtained Askham in 1375. On the south side is a wing 22m long by 10m wide over walls up to 1.7m thick. The south windows and two internal divisions date from a remodelling c1700 but the staircase and a doorway in the north wall are original and the basement has a tunnel-vault. The length of this building suggests that each of the three levels must have always been subdivided. Both northern corners have blocked latrine shutes, suggesting a layout with private chambers at either end of a living room or hall on the second storey. A hall block north of this wing was rebuilt in the 1570s by Thomas Sandford, being given a five-light window and a projecting bay on the west side. Also of that period are the much-altered ranges around the north and west sides of a court to the west, the latter containing an entrance passage. A staircase lobby of c1700 now occupies much of the former hall. The north wing beyond the hall block is also late 14th century but is much smaller and less massively built than the south wing. It contains rooms on either side of a passage through to the late 16th century kitchen, beyond which is some more medieval work and a range of c1700. The upper storey of the north wing is said to have contained a chapel. Askham Hall has been the seat of Lord Lonsdale since the dismantling of nearby Lowther Castle in 1957.

## BEAUMONT MOTTE   NY 348592   F

The summit of a motte on the site of Roman Milecastle 70a measures 28m by 37m and is occupied by a church containing 12th century work and its graveyard. Houses lie on the site of a bailey about 55m long by 46m wide to the NE. The de la Ferte had their seat here. It passed to a cousin, Richard le Brun, in 1300 and was probably abandoned after his grandson transferred to Drumburgh not long afterwards.

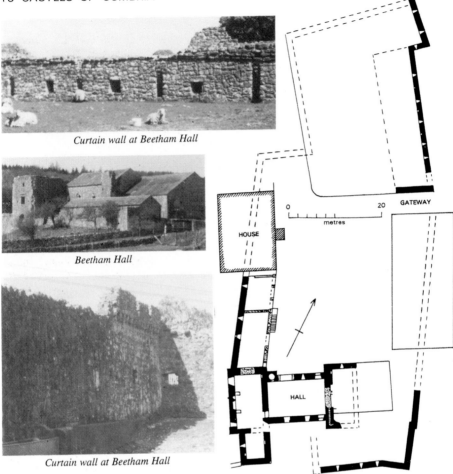

*Curtain wall at Beetham Hall*

*Beetham Hall*

*Curtain wall at Beetham Hall*

*Plan of Beetham Hall*

# BEETHAM HALL SD 499791

Parts of a loopholed curtain wall about 1m thick surround an irregularly shaped court 90m long by 36m wide. The gateway lay in the middle of the east side and on the west opposite it stands a house with the initials T.B with the date 1653 on the moulded lintel of a doorway. An outbuilding set against the curtain joins this house to the western cross-wing of the original house, which is ruined and much overgrown. This west wing contained a solar reached up from the hall by a staircase in the hall NW corner. South of the solar is a two storey block containing on the upper level a chapel (orientated almost south-north) with a piscina and fine end window. The hall windows are blocked or altered. To the east was a service wing similar in size to the solar wing. It has been ruined since the hall was taken from the Royalists by Thomas Fairfax in 1644. The service wing contained at least one upper chamber reached from the hall by a straight stair in the wing west wall which runs up to the base of a spiral stair in the SW corner. Probably there was also a third storey and battlements. Long held by the Beethams, the hall went to the Stanleys in 1485. It later passed to the Cliffords and then to the Wilsons of Dallam in 1767.

# BEWCASTLE CASTLE    NY 565748

William II probably founded this castle during his campaign of 1092 and it seems to have been placed in the custody of a Saxon or Danish lord called Bueth, hence its name. His grandson Robert was forfeited for siding with the Scots in 1174. The manor was later acquired by the de Levington family. The curtain wall may have been built after Bewcastle was sold in the 1270s to John de Swinburne, Sheriff of Cumberland. Adam de Swinburne was forfeited for supporting John Balliol in 1296 but was later restored to his possessions. Bewcastle later passed by marriage to John de Strivelyn, Constable of Edinburgh Castle. A stone from the castle showing his arms is built into an adjacent farm building. The castle is first mentioned on his death in 1378. The de Middletons inherited Bewcastle in 1391 but allowed it to decay. The castle and manor had been "long lying waste" when granted in 1470 by Edward IV to his brother Richard, Duke of Gloucester. The gatehouse may have been added either then or c1520 after a plan to demolish the castle and build a new stronghold at Arthuret was abandoned, although it could be the barbican mentioned as under construction in 1540-2, when the ditches were also deepened and the buildings repaired. In 1565 a survey records that the ditches were filling up with earth and mud and that on the north side a 15m long section of the decayed curtain wall had fallen. Repairs estimated at £320 were never executed. In 1614 the manor and castle were leased to the Earl of Cumberland but in 1629 they were granted to the Grahams of Netherby. The curtain wall must have been patched up for there was a garrison of 100 men stationed in the castle in 1639. Local tradition of the castle being damaged in the 1640s by a Parliamentary battery sited at "Cannon Holes" is partly borne out by cannon balls having been found in and around the site.

The castle lies in the NE corner of a Roman fort and has a ditch on the south and west sides. It consists of a court about 23m square enclosed by a wall 1.8m thick above a plinth. The north and east sides are very fragmentary but the south side still has a wall-walk 9m above ground and the west side is fairly complete too. On the south side stood a block containing a hall on the upper storey where two chimney flues and a pair of blocked Tudor windows remain. There were lean-to buildings, perhaps of timber, around the other sides. The gatehouse or barbican (it may not have been roofed) is 7.6m wide and projects 5.7m from the west wall. The outer arch lies on the north side and is shielded from the west by a big buttress on the NW corner. Because of the difficulty of turning a horse and cart in a short space, a right-angled turn as we have here is rare in the main entrance of an English castle. Steps up in the gatehouse west wall lead round the corner to a latrine on the south side.

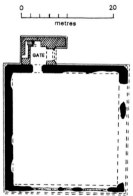

*Plan of Bewcastle*                    *Bewcastle*

Bewley Castle

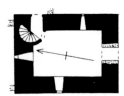

Brackenhill: plan of tower

0                                              10

metres

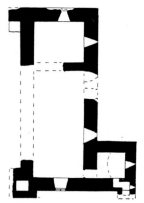

Plan of Bewley Castle

## BEWLEY CASTLE   NY 648212

This building erected c1325-32 by Bishop John Ross bears the name of Hugh de Beaulieu (pronounced Bewley), Bishop of Carlisle from 1219, who is said to have had a house here. Bishop William Strickland in the early 1400s re-roofed the chapel and the "lord's chamber", From the late 15th century until the early 18th the Machel family lived here as tenants. It was ruinous by 1774 when held by the Musgraves, and was finally sold by the Church Commissioners in 1857. The building comprises a block 19.2m long by 8.3m wide over walls 1.4m thick. The north end has a vaulted room with loops to the east and north. The rest formed one large chamber with a doorway and two loops facing east and a two-light window in the south end wall. A doorway leads into a vaulted room in the base of a wing 5.2m wide projecting 4.2m from the south end of the east wall. This small room has access to a latrine projecting on the south. The upper levels had latrines in a turret 3m square clasping the SW corner. The short length of walling 1.4m thick extending west from the NW corner suggests another chamber extending towards the stream. It has been suggested that Bewley was a courtyard castle but the remains do not seem to be part of such a plan.

## BIRDOSWALD   NY 615664   E

The west gate of the Roman fort remained standing into the medieval period and a tower 7m square over walls 1.6m thick was built 4.5m east of it. The Tweddales later replaced the tower by a bastle 10.5m by 6.5m further east. The bastle had a west doorway and double walls at the far end, perhaps to support an upper fireplace. Another bastle-like building to the north is incorporated in a 19th century house.

*Footings of tower at Birdoswald*

*Plan of Blencow Hall*

*Blencow Hall*

## BLENCOW HALL   NY 449326   V

The house consists of a habitable hall range with mullioned windows, dated 1590 over the entrance, and low ruined towers at each end. The south tower was bult by Sir Henry Blencow in the early 17th century but the north tower is probably late 15th century and measures 11.7m by 7.2m over walls 1.2m thick. It has a spiral stair in one corner but little remains of the battlements. The basement is subdivided and unvaulted. The original seat of the Blencow family is said to have been a tower on the other side of the River Petterell west of the fishponds at NY 458327.

## BRACKENBURGH TOWER   NY 476384

The house is mostly of 1907 by Sir Robert Lorimer but behind it are parts of an older house of 1852 itself incorporating a tower 11.7m by 7.8m over walls 1.5m thick.

## BRACKENHILL TOWER   NY 445695

By the River Lyne is a tower measuring 10.3m by 7.7m over walls 1.5m thick. It has a vaulted basement and a spiral stair in the NE corner with an east facing doorway at its foot. The south doorway is old but not original. The top is finished in the Scottish manner with a roof with stepped gables surrounded by a corbelled parapet rising 10.5m above ground. In 1596 Thomas Musgrave, Captain of Bewcastle, "being chased by the Scots, sought refuge here, but the gates were shut against him so he was caught". Richard Graham's widow proved in 1605 that his father had bought the tower from Sir Thomas Dacre. It was sold in 1752 to Roland Stephenson.

## BRAMPTON MOTTE   NY 532612   F

A statue of 1870 of the 7th Earl of Carlisle lies on a motte east of the village. It is set on a ridge high above the surrounding ground and has a ditch 6m wide with a counterscarp bank 2.5m high about 12m below the summit measuring 38m by 14m.

## BRANTHWAITE HALL    NY 065254

The tower measures 9.8m by 8.2m over walls 1.5m thick and is well preserved with a vaulted basement, several small original blocked windows, a parapet and a stair turret at the SE corner covered by a saddle-back roof. The block on the east side may have medieval masonry, and a projection on the south side has a 16th century window with arched heads to the lights. The mullioned windows with hood-moulds on the same side are of 1604. The north side was remodelled c1700 with five bays of mullion-and-transom windows with diagonally fanning-out lintel-stones on the lower storey and semicircular pediments on the upper storey. The National Coal Board restored the house in 1984 but put it up for sale in 1992.

*Branthwaite: plan and view*

## BROUGH    NY 792141    E F

This castle lies in the northern part of a rectangular platform assumed to be the site of the Roman fort of Verterae. The castle was founded by William II in 1092 and may have been of stone from the beginning since parts of the curtains are obviously of early date. In 1174 the castle was captured and destroyed by the Scots under William the Lion and the keep is assumed to have been built by Henry II soon afterwards. King John repaired the castle between 1199 and 1202 but in 1204 he granted it to Robert de Vipont. His son succeeded as a minor and in 1228 the castle was held by the Justiciar, Hubert de Bugh, acting as guardian. In 1245 the castle was in need of repair and works subsequently carried out included the rebuilding of the central section of the north curtain and the provision of a new gatehouse on the south side. By that time the castle had passed to the Cliffords and Edward I and Edward II both stayed when travelling between York and Carlisle. The Scots burnt the adjacent town in 1314 after the English defeat at Bannockburn, and again in 1319, but the castle appears to have held out. Robert, 1st Lord Clifford had strengthened it c1300, rebuilding the east curtain and adding the round tower that bears his name.

*Brough Castle*

Later in the 14th century Roger, 5th Lord Clifford, built a new hall block between the gatehouse and Clifford's Tower. The 9th Lord Clifford, a Lancastrian noted for severity towards the Yorkists, was killed in the battle of Towton in 1461, and Brough was later held by Richard Neville, Earl of Warwick, "The Kingmaker". The 10th Lord Clifford was raised in secret as a shepherd on his father's former estates and only regained Brough after Henry Tudor defeated Richard III at Bosworth. He often lived at the castle, despite having several other residences.

In 1521 the castle caught fire during a Christmas feast and is said to have remained in ruins until it was restored in 1659-62 by the Lady Anne Clifford, Countess Dowager of Pembroke, Dorset and Montgomery, and the last of Cliffords to own Brough. She built the range, probably a stable block, west of the gateway, and rebuilt Clifford's Tower, only for it to be again gutted by fire in 1666. The castle was abandoned not long afterwards, materials being removed for reuse at Appleby. The keep was roofless by 1695 and the fittings of the domestic buildings were sold in 1714. Brough Mill was repaired with stone from Clifford's Tower in the 1760s. In 1923 the ruins were handed placed in state care as an ancient monument.

*Brough Castle*

*Brough Castle*

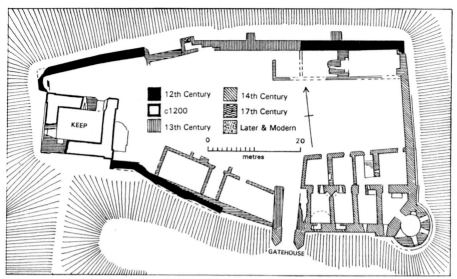

*Plan of Brough Castle*

The castle has a single court 75m long from east to west by 35m wide at the east end but narrowing to about 19m at the west end. There is a gatehouse about 7.5m wide on the south side with a hall-block connecting it to Clifford's Tower at the SE corner. The gateway passage has 11th or 12th century masonry on the west side and a stair rises in the wall thickness on the east. Much of the building is late 13th century but the keel-shaped buttresses facing the field are late 14th century. The hall has two windows formerly of two lights on the south side and lay above three rooms with vaults rebuilt or inserted in 1659-62. The western two lower rooms have latrines in the outer wall. The eastern room contains a service stair. In front of the hall block lay a small forecourt which was subdivided into chambers in 1659-62. The hall stair then inserted blocks a loop in a wall which is a relic of an earlier hall block built against the east curtain. Excavations have shown that this replaced an earlier timber hall. Clifford's Tower is of three storeys and has a straight face of c1300 towards the court. The round outer part about 8.5m in diameter is 17th century work above the stepped plinth and has mullioned windows typical of that period. Not much remains of a 17th century kitchen range built against the eastern end of the north curtain and the stables against the SW curtain. Over the stables were lofts for grooms reached by an open stair from the court. The projections from the north curtain wall, one with a latrine shute, are late 13th century. There is a mural stair in the NW corner.

The keep measures 14.6m long by 12m wide and is a building of c1180 on the site of an older tower, foundations of which remain visible on the northern side. Original features are the clasping corner buttresses and one window of two lights at third storey level. The entrance into the storage basement is 17th century and originally access was only by means of an open stair against the east end wall to a doorway into the hall on the second storey. A straight stair in this end wall then led to the private chamber on the third storey, from which a spiral stair in the NE corner gave access to the battlements. The original roof was screened by the upper parts of the walls but later on this space was used as an extra chamber. The SE corner of the keep fell down in 1792 (it has been patched up in modern times). Despite having been rebuilt in the 17th century the SW corner also collapsed in 1920.

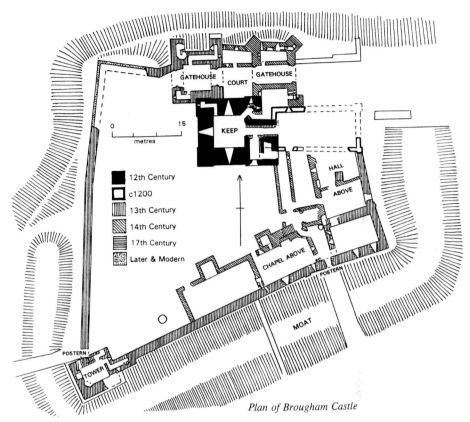

*Plan of Brougham Castle*

# BROUGHAM CASTLE   NY 537290   E

It is uncertain when or by whom this castle occupying the northern side of a Roman fort was founded. It may have been built by Gospatric, son of Orm, to whom an estate here was granted by Henry II after he recovered Cumbria from the Scottish kings. The keep is assumed to date from the 1170s or 80s and soon afterwards the castle passed to the Vipont family who built a block east of the keep. In the mid 13th century a Vipont heiress married Roger de Clifford, who was killed during the conflicts of 1263-5. Their son inherited Brougham and built the curtain walls, whilst his son Robert, who built the tower at the SW corner of the court and the gatehouse north of the keep, was killed in the English defeat at Bannockburn in 1314. Robert's grandson Roger was executed by Edward II after the battle of Boroughbridge in 1322. Roger, 5th Lord Clifford remodelled the domestic apartments in the late 14th century. The last of this line was Lady Anne Clifford, Dowager Countess of Pembroke, Dorset and Montgomery. On the outer gatehouse is a slab recording her many titles and giving a biblical quotation which is a reference to her work in restoring Brougham and her other seats which had become ruinous. After her death in 1676 Brough passed to the Earls of Thanet. They had little interest in antiquated northern seats like Brougham and in 1714 the building was stripped of its lead and timber and abandoned. In the mid 19th century the estate passed to the Tufton family, one of whom, as 3rd Lord Hothfield, placed the ruins in state care for preservation in 1928.

The castle has a spear-head shaped court with the 65m long south side and the 59m long west side meeting at a sharp angle from which projects the late 13th century Tower of League. This building contained four storeys of lodgings with latrines and fireplaces and stands high except for the collapsed eastern corner. The upper levels are linked by a spiral stair in a round turret projected out on the northern side. The lowest level has cross-shaped arrow-loops facing west and north. The west wall of the court is defaced on the inside, where there were once bakehouses and other service rooms, and the external facing is 17th century. A low modern wall fills a breach at the NW corner. Beside the tower is a postern which is 17th century in its present form and not far away is a well. The south wall of the court is better preserved. It too has a 17th century doorway leading to a causeway across the dry moat. Built against this wall are a very ruined early 14th century block of lodgings and a late 14th century block containing a chapel over an office or apartment. The chapel has windows and sedilia and piscina all with trefoiled heads in the south wall and the lower part of a big east window. It was reached by an external stair on the north side rising to a small porch with a tiny chamber below it.

The chapel staircase ascended from a lobby from which also rose a stair up to the hall in the east range. The south end of the range contained a kitchen and one further upper room above a pantry covered by a ribbed barrel-vault and having a service stair against its east wall. Between this room and the chapel block was a tiny court containing a well and the postern already noted. There was also a tiny court west of the hall, the west side of which was closed by a late 14th century corridor connecting the central lobby to the keep. East of the keep and north of the 14th century hall-block was a rather more thinly walled block of c1200-20, now destroyed except for its west end and the SE corner with a clasping buttress. The range may have originally been built as a hall, with the keep serving as its solar block, but at one time it had a third storey containing a chapel and by the late 14th century its second storey formed the solar.

*Tower of League, Brougham Castle*

*Brougham: the keep*

*Brougham: section of keep*

*Hall block at Brougham Castle*

The keep measures 13.2m by 14m over walls 3.3m thick and has broad and flat clasping corner buttresses. It originally had three storeys and was entered at the level of the hall on the second storey by means of a stair in a forebuilding on the east side. The basement has loops on the other three sides, a spiral stair to all the levels in the NE corner, and a latrine in the NW corner. The latrine suggests this room was not the usual cellar. It was later given a ribbed vault with a central octagonal pier and a passage cut through towards the block on the east. A fourth storey added c1300 has a main room with chamfered corners on squinch arches to provide space for mural chambers in the corners. That at the SE is a polygonal oratory with a ribbed vault and recesses and a piscina. A passage connects these chambers with the staircase.

At the end of the 13th century a gatehouse about 10.7m square was added to the NW corner of the keep. The gateway passage is vaulted and was closed by portcullises at each end. A long passage leads from the gateway hall to a latrine in a turret at the east end of the north wall. Another turret at the west end of the wall contains a spiral stair leading down from the chambers above to a postern. About a generation later a second gatehouse was added against the NE corner of the keep and still later a thinly walled range was built on the north side of the small court between the two gatehouses. The outer gate contained two storeys of fine upper rooms with latrines and windows with quatrefoil tracery and transoms above a passage with inner and outer portcullises. There are turrets diagonally projecting from the northern corners of this building. The single room on the top storey was known as the Painted Chamber in the time of the Lady Anne Clifford.

*Brougham, plan of keep*

*Brougham Castle*

## BROUGHTON TOWER    NY 214879

In the mid 18th century the Gilpin Sawreys built a mansion around an 18m high 14th century tower measuring 12.6m by 9.4m over walls 1.9m thick. A thicker southern section of the east wall contains the entrance and an adjoining spiral stair in the SE corner. There are two vaults of unequal size in the basement, the larger room having two original loops. Wings were added to the mansion in 1882. An early 16th century portal in the hall is from France. There is an Italian Renaissance chimneypiece in the dining room. The de Broctons were here from the 12th century until they were forfeited and their lands given to the Earl of Derby in 1487. The tower was sold to the Leighs in 1653 and then to the Sawreys in 1658.

*Plan of Burneside Hall*

## BURGH-BY-SANDS    NY 314592

Nothing now remains of a castle at the west end of the village but excavations in 1950 found evidence of four periods of building. The site lies across a robbed-out portion of Hadrian's Wall. A ditched motte erected probably c1100 by Robert de Trevers passed by marriage c1120 to Ranulph Engaine. He or his son William seem to have levelled the motte and replaced it by a grange on a rectangular ditched platform. After William died c1158 Burgh passed by marriage to Simon de Morville. He or his son Hugh built a curtain wall 2.2m thick. After Hugh died in 1202 the castle went firstly to Richard de Lucy of Egremont and then to Thomas de Multon. This family replaced the curtain by a hall-block 15.5m long by 10.4m wide to the NW corner of which a round tower 7.6m in diameter was later added. When the castle passed by marriage to Ranulph Dacre c1314 it was said to be "a capital messuage worth 24 shillings". It is assumed to have been destroyed by a Scottish raid not long afterwards for by 1362 it was "a ruin worth nothing". A tower added at the west end of the church seems to have replaced it as a strongpoint for the defence of the village. Ruins of the castle survived until the early 17th century.

*Burneside Hall*

*Burneside: gatehouse*

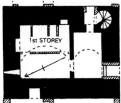

*Plan of Broughton Tower*

*Burneside Hall*

## BURNESIDE HALL   SD 510960

Burneside belonged to the Burneshead and Bellingham families until the 16th century. The house is essentially 14th century and consists of a much altered central hall with north and south cross-wings which in a drawing of c1692 are both shown as having three storeys and battlements. The north wing, now ruinous, formed a tower 12.8m long by 8.5m wide over walls mostly about 1.2m thick. The basement contained two vaulted rooms set either side of a passage leading out to a thinly walled enclosure 11m square on the north side. A stair in the tower south wall led directly from the hall to the solar. The hall is now divided into a kitchen at the north end, a parlour with 17th century fireplace, and a staircase at the south end. The south wing is 22.3m long and has three parts each of differing widths. The central part seems to have been a kitchen with a huge fireplace filling the south side. West of the house is a 16th century gatehouse with an 8m long section of curtain wall 1.9m thick complete with parapet curving round from the north side. Low modern walls connect these parts to the hall to enclose a court with three sides each about 28m long.

## CAERNARVON CASTLE   NY 021072 & 010081

The original seat of the le Fleming family in this area seems to have been the 4m high motte with traces of a small kidney shaped bailey at Wodobank. The summit measures 9m across and has been damaged by a former railway. Richard le Fleming, who died c1207 is described as of Caernarvon Castle, Beckermet, so by then the family had transferred to the rectangular ditched enclosure there which is now very worn but seems to have been 92m long by 77m wide with a ditch 11m wide. The site was probably abandoned c1250 when the le Flemings moved to Coniston. The name Caernarvon means "the castle over against Mona (Isle of Man)".

## CAPPLESIDE HALL   SD 501804

The south side of a 15th century tower 11.4m by 7.8m over walls 1.1m thick remains in a barn. It has projections at each end, that to the west containing latrines. There was a spiral stair in the NE corner with a north facing entrance beside it. A hall block to the north with a kitchen beyond were dismantled in 1687 after the house passed by marriage to the Cliffords. It was previously held by the Prestons, passing to the Middletons in 1585, and then going to the Buskells and the Orbells.

## CARLISLE CASTLE    NY 397562    E

In 1092 William II, known as "Rufus" came north to drive out Dolfin, the Saxon ruler of this district. He then chose a bluff on the south side of the River Eden as a fine site on which to build a castle which is generally assumed to have been of earth and wood. In 1136 King Stephen was forced to let King David of Scotland rule Cumbria. David is generally thought to have built the stone keep although there is no evidence that similar towers of this period existed in his other domains. King David died in the castle in 1153 and in 1157 his successor Malcolm returned Cumbria to Henry II of England. It was probably Henry II that first walled the inner ward in stone, and perhaps the outer ward too, although the walls there could be as late as King John's reign. In 1173 Henry II's sons rebelled against him and offered possession of Carlisle to the Scottish king, William the Lion in return for his support. William advanced on Carlisle but retired when he heard an English army was coming to support it. In 1174 he returned with a large army and laid siege to several border castles, including Carlisle. After three months Robert de Vaux and his garrison were in a desperate state but then the siege was raised by the Scottish king being defeated and captured at Alnwick. There are records of repairs to the castle by Richard I and King John. Alexander II of Scotland is also said to have repaired the defences after he captured the castle in 1216 on his second attempt during the civil wars at the end of King's John's reign, but the crack from top to bottom in the fabric of the outer gatehouse reported in a survey of 1257 may have been a relic of damage sustained in the siege.

*The keep, Carlisle Castle*

*Carlisle Castle from the SE*

Edward I made frequent use of the castle both as a fortress and residence and held three parliaments within it. The accounts of the keeper John de Halton refer to repairs on the great hall, kitchens, stores and stable. Glass was purchased for the windows of the king's chamber and chapel and large stocks of military stores were acquired, including timber, iron, steel and brass for building siege engines for use on the king's campaigns in Scotland. Edward II was much less able as a military leader than his father and by 1311 King Robert (the Bruce) of Scotland was able to blockade de Halton's garrison in Carlisle Castle. Bruce won a great victory over Edward II at Bannockburn in the summer of 1314 and a few months later he attacked Carlisle, the siege being vividly described in the Chronicle of Lanercost Priory. Both sides used catapults but it was claimed that those belonging to the defenders were more effective. The Scots then tried to breach the walls with an engine called a sow and also to scale them with ladders but both attempts failed. A huge wheeled tower or belfry was brought up close to the castle to command the walls but it got stuck in mud and failed in its purpose. Although the surrounding country was pillaged the castle remained untaken. The commander Sir Andrew de Harcla was treated as a hero and in 1322 was created Earl of Carlisle and Lord Warden of the Marches. Not long afterwards he was involved with negotiations with the Scots but his enemies at court managed to use this a pretext for accusing him of treason. He was arrested within Carlisle Castle by Sir Anthony de Lucy, Sheriff of Cumberland, and unjustly stripped of his honours and hanged, drawn and quartered as a traitor.

In 1378 the young Richard II had work begun on a new outer gatehouse which still remains. The Scots twice attacked Carlisle during Richard II's reign but failed to take the castle. In the 1470s Edward IV sent his brother Richard, Duke of Gloucester to command the Marches. Considerable repairs were executed to the defences and domestic buildings during this period. During Henry VIII's reign the Dacre family were Wardens of the Western Marches and Captains of Carlisle Castle. At Cardinal Wolsey's instigation they carried out several raids into Scotland. The castle defences were improved and adapted for defence by cannon including provision of a long-vanished outer line of defence on the NE side, and the city defences were strengthened by the erection of the citadel at the south end. Depite this the castle was reported to be in need of repairs early in Elizabeth I's reign, a 20m long section of the outer ward wall having fallen in 1557. The fugitive Mary, Queen of Scots was accommodated in the now destroyed suite of two upper rooms in the former SE corner tower of the castle for two months after she fled from Scotland in 1568.

*Portcullis of outer gate, Carlisle Castle*

The reputation of the castle as an almost impregnable stronghold was somewhat shattered by an incident in 1596. One night Sir Walter Scott with a force of about 200 men rode to Carlisle, breached the postern gate in the middle of the west wall of the outer ward, and released his kinsman William Armstrong of Kinmont, a notorious castle reiver who was imprisoned probably in the basement of a tower thought to have once stood in the SW corner of the outer ward.

After the city of York surrendered to Parliamentary forces in 1644, Sir Thomas Glenham, commander of King Charles's forces in the north, fled to Carlisle and was besieged there by General Leslie. The garrison only surrendered after the Royalist defeat at Naseby in June 1645. Considerable repairs to the castle and city defences were required after this siege and in their haste to obtain stone to patch the walls the Scots demolished most of the nave of the cathedral in addition to the cloisters, chapter-house and the canons' houses. Sir Philip Musgrave managed to obtain possession of the castle for King Charles in 1648. It was surrendered to Cromwellian troops after their victory at Preston and a force of 800 foot and 1200 horse was sent by Cromwell to hold the castle and carry out raids into Scotland.

When a Jacobite force led by Prince Charles Edward Stuart arrived at Carlisle in 1745 the castle was defended by two officers, four gunners and eighty "invalides" (old or infirm men past serious military service), plus 700 poorly trained and inadequately equipped men of the Cumberland and Westorland militias. This weak force was disinclined to fight and pursuaded Colonel Durand to submit after a siege of seven days, the details being recorded by the Colonel's subsequent court-martial. The prince proclaimed his father as rightful King of England at Carlisle Cross the following day and then marched south leaving a small garrison. By Christmas the prince had retreated to Carlisle. He left 400 Highlanders to defend the castle against the Duke of Cumberland. They were soon forced to submit after the Duke's artillery arrived from Whitehaven. After the final Jacobite defeat at Culloden many of the captured rebels were incarcerated at Carlisle prior to being hanged or transported. The castle remained in use as a military garrison and depot until 1962. It became an ancient monument with public access in 1927 and a museum of the Border Regiment was then established in the keep.

The walled city was a lozenge of nearly 45 acres with the River Eden on the north and the Petterill and Caldew streams on the east and west sides. Henry VIII's citadel incorporated the Bochard Gate at the south end. The Richard or Scottish gate on the east and the Caldew or Irish gate near the north end of the west side have gone but fragments of the walls remain, especially above the railway on the west side. The walls were built near the top of the slopes of the ridge so that their height on the inner side was much less than their height towards the field. The castle lies at the north end on a ridge 18m above the Eden. The walls enclose a wedge-shaped area with the sharp edge of the wedge divided off to form an inner ward. There is a deep ditch on the south side of the castle and originally there was a second ditch further south with a palisade on the inner edge of it. Reached from the open space or glacis thus enclosed by this ditch and the city walls was the Tile Tower, a rectangular structure originally of the same date as the late 12th or 13th century city walls but partly rebuilt in brick by Richard III, whose crest of a white boar appears on a stone on the south side. The tower has a living room with a fireplace and latrine set above a lower room with three arrow-loops, both levels being vaulted in brick.

Rebuilding during the 19th century has ironically done more harm to the ancient buildings than several hundred years of Scottish sieges. No traces of old buildings remain in the outer ward where in the 19th century the ground was raised to make a tarmac-covered parade ground flanked by large new barrack-blocks. The walls themselves have been much patched and remodelled, especially at the top, none of present parapets being earlier than the 18th century. As a result of adaptation to take cannon all the walls and buildings have a cut-down appearance. On the north side there is just one slight projection near the west end. A bastion about 14m wide probably of the 1540s, later part a battery, covers the polygonal NW corner. On the west side lies the 15th century postern breached during the rescue of "Kinmont Willie" in 1596 with a rectangular tower a short distance north of it. The parts of the tower which stood above the main wall-walk have been removed. A similar fate must have befallen the supposed tower at the SW corner (it does not appear on a mid 16th century plan). In later years this corner had a battery mounting four cannon.

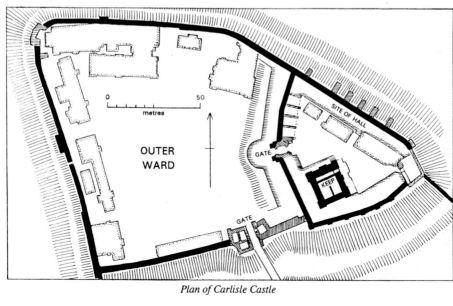

*Plan of Carlisle Castle*

By far the most interesting feature of the outer ward is the gatehouse on the south side known as De Ireby's Tower. This was built by the mason John Lewyn under the terms of a still-surviving contract made with Richard II in April 1378, and the name seems to have been inherited from the previous gatehouse damaged in the siege of 1216. As was commonly the case the tower was named after the landowner whose men were to defend it in times of war. The building has a two storey main block 15m long containing a hall and chamber over a gateway passage with two vaulted guard rooms west of it, the further of the two once having access to a latrine. The passage still has a portcullis in the outer arch. The hall is reached by a straight stair up from a doorway in the north wall. On the south side is a projecting wing which contained a kitchen over a room with a latrine (originally accessible directly from the entrance passage) which itself lies over a prison which could only have been reached by a trap-door. East of this wing is a barbican which at the level of the upper storey has a wall-walk with a parapet (renewed in the 18th century) on both sides so that defenders could look down from all four sides onto what was effectively a small open court in front of the main gateway. The three storey square block adjoining on the east side lies at an awkward angle to the rest and must incorporate at least in its lower portions part of the 13th century gatehouse which is likely to have comprised a central passage flanked by square towers projecting mostly within the courtyard. This part has its own entrance and has a straight stair rising in the north wall to a spiral stair in the NE corner. The second storey room has a passage (originally a latrine) from a window embrasure leading out to the curtain wall-walk. A doorway on the east side of the barbican led to a building added on the outer side of the curtain wall here in the 15th or 16th century, and destroyed by the 18th century.

*Inner gatehouse, Carlisle Castle*

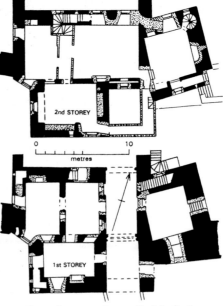

*Plans of outer gatehouse, Carlisle Castle*

The triangular inner ward has a slightly bowed south side about 60m long with a series of flat buttresses and projects beyond the line of the outer ward curtain so as to flank it. The straight NE side is 80m long and has a series of closely spaced massive buttresses added during the 16th or 18th centuries. At the east corner between the two sides was a three storey tower, originally a 12th century gatehouse since a blocked round arch is clearly shown on old prints, but probably not used as such after rebuilding in the late 14th century. It was later named after Mary, Queen of Scots, who stayed within it in 1568. The tower was mostly replaced in the 1830s by a simple new corner to the curtain and the principal relic of it is a polygonal stair turret with some ornamental arcading which stood at its NW corner. The west curtain facing the outer ward is 70m long and has a square gatehouse in the middle where the curtain makes an angle. There is a ditch in front of this side which, like the ditch on the south side of the castle, was originally water filled and stocked with fish. In front of the gatehouse is a half-moon battery of the 1540s. The lower part contains a loopholed passage commanding the lower part of the ditch, while the upper part, once taller, had three guns mounted upon it. A breastwork ran parallel to the curtain to a gate beside the outer ward wall where there was a drawbridge across the moat, later replaced by a permanent stone bridge.

*Stair turret of Queen Mary's Tower, Carlisle*

The three storey inner gatehouse or Captain's Tower is mostly 14th century but the plain pointed arch above the outer portal and its flanking buttresses are thought to be late 12th century, and there are considerable later additions. A portcullis groove still survives at the east end of the passage and also blocked machicolations. Over this eastern arch is an outer arch decorated with cusped foils with figures supporting shields. One shield has the arms of Robert Neville, entrusted by Edward III to oversee repairs at the castle. Beside a doorway to a cellar south of the passage is a fleur-de-lis graffiti dated 1521.

The inner ward has a very cluttered appearence. The keep stands within the SW corner and abutting against the NE side are 19th century buildings on the site of the former great hall and private chambers. From the 1540s onwards much of the courtyard space was filled when the walls were thickened internally and casemates built against them to provide a wide fighting platform upon which cannon could be mounted on all sides. The thick parapet with wide ports for cannon dates from this period and later. A long ramp with slight steps was built up alongside the north face of the keep and a new arch built against the inner side of the gatehouse to allow easy access at wall-walk level from one side of it to the other, the original pedestrian doorways through the third storey being inadequate for the manhandling of artillery.

The keep measures 20m from north to south by 18m from east to west but the south wall seems to have been rebuilt thinner so the keep may have originally been another metre longer. An outside stair against the east wall once led up to an entrance at the south end of the east wall. In later years this doorway communicated with a range built in 1577 but mostly demolished in 1812. The doorway led into a hall with windows facing south and west, a fireplace on the east, a latrine in the SW corner, and mural rooms in the north wall, one of which had access to a well. In the NW corner is a spiral stair which originally connected all three storeys and the battlements. A straight stair leads down to a 14th century entrance at ground level, that now in use. This was closed by a portcullis operated from a chamber above. Originally the basement was undivided but this entrance now leads into a passage at the north end off which open two vaulted cellars, one running the length of the keep, the other only half the length but with a third cellar opening off it. The crosswalls and vaults and the blocking of all but one of the original six loops lighting the basement seems to be work of the 1570s, following a report by Lord Scrope to Elizabeth I that the keep was badly cracked. The crosswalls of the two original upper storeys and the addition of the vaulted topmost storey are also of that period whilst the existing massive parapets are of 1812 when flagstones were laid on the vaults and cannon mounted on top. Originally a lordly residence, by the 15th century the keep served only as a lookout point, storehouse and prison. Mural rooms in the east wall at third storey level contain prisoners' carvings going back to that period.

## CARLISLE CITADEL   NY 601558    V

The citadel built for Henry VIII in 1541-3 by the German engineer Stefan von Haschenperg to augment the defences at the south end of the city featured the medieval Bochard Gate in the middle with a U-shaped bastion behind it. A plain new gateway called the English Gate was provided nearby to the west. On the east and west sides of the old gatehouse were triangular artillery platforms with the outermost corners occupied by round bastions about 15m in diameter over walls more than 3m thick. The eastern of the two round bastions survives within the Assize Courts of 1805-11, the interior of the bastion housing the Nisi Prius courtroom.

*Carlisle Citadel*

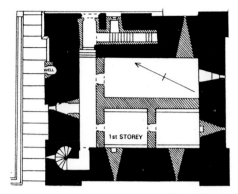
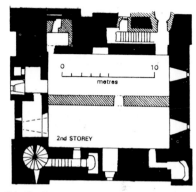

*Plans of keep of Carlisle Castle*

# CARLISLE DEANERY   NY 598559   V

The core of the deanery is a tower built c1510-20 by Prior Simon Senhouse, the moulded beams of a ceiling having an inscription referring to him. The tower measures 9.8m by 9.3m over walls 1.8m thick and contained a fine upper room with north and south oriels set above a tunnel-vaulted basement with five closely set chamfered transverse arches. The third storey may be a later insertion. To the west is a hall range with a kitchen with a huge fireplace, and there is a Georgian wing to the east. Beyond that lay the Bishop's Tower, probably built in the 14th century, still standing in 1620, but probably demolished in the 1640s. A map of the 1560s suggests it formed part of the western range of the monastic buildings.

# CASTLE CARROCK   NY 544554

In the 1160 Gamel de Castlecarrock had his seat either on the platform 90m by 45m with a 6m wide ditch immediately east of the church, or at the very worn ringwork 52m diameter on the much higher ground of Jacobs Hill at 544556. The family became extinct in Edward I's reign. There is a tradition of masonry being removed.

# CASTLE CRAG   NY 469128

High above Haweswater is a crag made into a ringwork 14m by 8m rising 5.5m above a rock-cut ditch 3m deep and 8m wide dividing it from a platform 15m by 7m to the SW. Excavations in 1922 found traces of a drystone parapet on the north side.

# CASTLE SOWERBY   NY 360383

The "castellum de Sourebi" mentioned in 1186-7 may have been the possible ringwork 19m across which formerly lay on the west bank of a stream, but is more likely to have been the now-overgrown motte and bailey site of Castle How 1.5km to the north. The motte there rises 12m from the ditch on the west to a summit 34m by 15m. A rock-cut ditch isolates it from a bailey 75m by 60m to the north, and there is a possible outer enclosure to the west and NW. The castle was founded either by the Scots in c1136-57 or by the de Vaux family in the 1120s or 1160s. The castle passed to the Crown when Robert de Vaux died in 1195 on account of an unpaid debt of £50. Probably then abandoned, it is not mentioned in the grant of the manor of 1213 to Robert de Roos, nor in another grant of 1237 to Alexander II of Scotland.

*Catterlen Hall*

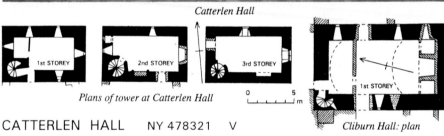

*Plans of tower at Catterlen Hall*

## CATTERLEN HALL   NY 478321   V

*Cliburn Hall: plan*

The north end of this L-shaped building is a medieval tower 8.7m by 5.9m over walls 1.2m thick. It has a spiral stair in the SW corner with a doorway adjoining facing south, and windows of two cusped lights under a square head. One window is later and larger. The corbels on the west seem to have been for supporting a wooden defensive platform. South of the tower is a hall-range of 1577 built by Roland Vaux with windows with arched lights and a later projection on the west containing a spiral stair. Projecting east from the hall-block south end is a wing of the 1650s built by Christopher Richmond, who married the heiress Mabel Vaux. It contains a large upper room with two chimney-pieces. It is reached by an external staircase up to an ornate Baroque doorway with a pedimental gable above. An older earthwork lies to the east.

## CLIBURN HALL   NY 598245

The mullion-and-transom windows provided in a rebuilding of the upper parts and addition of a stair wing by Richard Cliburn 1567 and the gabled roof of c1872 give a misleading impression, for this is a tower built by Robert de Cliburn c1387 measuring 13.8m by 8.8m over walls 1.7m thick. It has a segmental vault in the basement, which has several original loops and a fireplace flanked by small rooms at the south end. There is a spiral stair in the NW corner with an adjoining doorway facing north. In 1454 John Cliburn was besieged here by William de Thisteald, who shot over 1,000 arrows into the house. It was sold in 1654, passed quickly through the Collingwood, Sawrey and Lee families, and went in 1667 to Sir John Lowther.

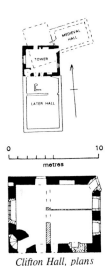

*Clifton Hall, plans*

*Clifton Hall*

## CLIFTON HALL   NY 531272   E

The three storey solar block with battlements stepped up at the corners now stands empty and alone but two doorways in the south wall show where the hall was until demolished c1800. The block measures 10.2m by 8m over walls 0.9m thick and probably dates from c1500. A spiral stair rises up in the SW corner and has a doorway at its foot. There are large 18th century windows in the east wall. Only the beams remain of the floor of the third storey. Traces of an earlier hall at an odd angle adjoin the NE corner. The Wybergh family lived here from 1365 until it passed to the Lowthers in 1705, having been mortgaged in the 1650s. The tower was captured by the Jacobites in 1715 and again in 1745. The 12th century church lies on top of what may be a low motte with a crescent shaped bailey to the NE.

*Old print of Cockermouth Castle*

# COCKERMOUTH CASTLE   NY 123308

An earthwork castle may have been built here after William, son of King Duncan II of Scotland married Alice de Rumeli of Skipton in the early 12th century. There was certainly a castle here in 1215 when their grandson William de Fortibus signed Magna Carta. It was ordered to be destroyed in 1221 but he later made his peace with those then ruling England for the young Henry III and rebuilding in stone began 1225 with the walling in of a modest triangular court on the tip of the strong promontory site. William's daughter-in-law Isabella died in possession of the castle in 1293. Edward I granted the castle to Thomas de Richmond in 1300, and Edward granted it to his favourite Piers Gaveston in 1309. Anthony de Lucy, a descendant of William FitzDuncan, obtained possesion in 1323. His son Thomas built a new suite of apartments on the NW side of the inner ward c1360. About twenty years later Thomas's daughter Maud and her first husband Gilbert de Umfraville, Earl of Angus extended the building by erecting a new outer wall not far in front of the east curtain, the space between the curtains being used for another range of apartments. Her second husband Henry Percy, created Earl of Northumberland in 1377, completed this range from 1385 onwards and rebuilt the outer ward after the castle was taken and wrecked by the Scots in 1387. Over the outer arch of the outer ward gatehouse are five coats of arms. From the left the first, third and fourth are those of the de Umfravilles, the de Lucys, and the Percies. The second is that of Maud's mother's family the de Multons, and the fifth for Margaret Neville, Henry Percy's second wife.

The first four earls of Northumberland all suffered violent deaths but Cockermouth was sufficiently remote both from the chief Percy seats at Alnwick and Warkworth and central England to be little affected by their struggles. However the Earl of Wiltshire and Dr John Morton are said to have been captured when the castle was taken by the Yorkists after their victory at Towton in 1461 in which the 3rd Earl of Northumberland was killed. The Earl of Wiltshire was executed but Morton survived to become a cardinal and Archbishop of Canterbury.

*Outer gatehouse at Cockermouth Castle*

In the 16th century the castle was little used by the Percies, and in 1530 the 6th Earl granted the 340 acre park to the NE beside the River Derwent to Thomas Wharton, the comptroller of his household. In 1567 and 1578 surveys reported the castle to be in need of urgent repairs, and when Mary, Queen of Scots stayed at Cockermouth in 1568 on her way to Carlisle from a landing at Workington she was accommodated in the hall in the market place rather than at the delapidated castle. The 1578 survey marked the return of the castle to the Percies after being confiscated in 1569, and it had previously been in Crown hands from 1537 to 1557. Sir Wilfred Lawson was keeper of the castle in 1605 and reported that his wife's son was living in the outer gatehouse, the rest of the buildings being ruinous.

During August and September 1648 a Parliamentary garrison under Lieutenant Bird was besieged here by 500 Royalists led by Sir Marmaduke Langdale. The garrison were negotiating terms for a surrender when news arrived of the Parliamentary victory at Preston and they held out until Lieutenant-Colonel Ashton arrived with a relieving force at the end of the month. The defences were slighted in the following year, the parapets being knocked off and the ditch in front of the inner ward filled in. Some of the lead roofs were also removed. By 1676 the only usable rooms were a dining room, kitchen, 4 bedrooms, stables, cellars, a bakehouse, and a courtroom in the Flagstaff tower at the SE corner.

In 1750 the Percies' Cumbrian estates passed to Charles Wyndham, 2nd Earl of Egremont. His successor erected new low domestic ranges against the walls of the outer court. The range on the east side was added by General Henry Wyndham, who lived in the castle from 1837 to 1860. It still belongs to this family. The last baron used the title of Lord Egremont given to him in 1963, but his original title was Lord Leconfield.

*Plan of Cockermouth Castle*

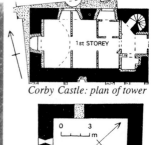

Corby Castle: plan of tower

Plan of Crew Castle

Inner ward of Cockermouth Castle

The castle has a superb defensive site on a promontory rising 20m above the confluence of the Derwent and Cocker rivers. Of the original castle of the late 1220s on the west end of the promontory all that remains is the lower part of the walling of the 7.6m diameter D-shaped tower at the west end and the adjoining walls. At the SE corner is the Bell Tower, a leaning structure 5m by 4m with the entrance of the original castle in the 3m thick east wall beside it. This wall appears to be of the 1360s, and of the same period are the apartments along the NW side of the court, with a hall 14.5m by 10m at the east end, and private apartments to the west. Towards the north these apartments raised over cellars or offices have one original late 14th century window and three others of three lights with transoms which are Elizabethan. The hall outer wall is supported by heavy buttresses of slightly later date.

Within twenty years of being rebuilt the east curtain became the inner wall of a new range of apartments with cellars within the original 13th century ditch, a new ditch being provided further east. The north end of the range is formed by the Kitchen Tower measuring 15.2m by 16.2m externally. The kitchen occupies the equivalant of two upper storeys over a cellar and has tall east windows, fireplaces in the south wall, a big modern arch towards the hall, and two loftly vaulted recesses (originally perhaps intended to be fireplaces?) in the slightly angled north wall. In front of the new range is a gatehouse with a high archway between two square towers with rib-vaulted guard-rooms flanking the passage. The archway has a machicolation and recalls a similar gatehouse of the same period at Castle Rushen on the Isle of Man.

Flagstaff Tower and outer curtain at Cockermouth Castle

The outer ward of c1390-1400 has a maximum width of 65m and extends 57m to the east beyond the new inner curtain. There are two small rectangular turrets on the south side and another on the east where the curtain makes a change of alignment. At the SE corner is the 9.4m square Flagstaff Tower near which in 1904 was revealed the base of a small round tower, evidence that the outer ward may have been fortified in stone in the 13th century. At the NE corner is the gatehouse, a block 15.2m long and 9.8m wide with projections at each end of the north and south walls. The latter contains a spiral stair with an umbrella-vault of eight ribs at the top. In front of the gatehouse extends a contemporary barbican.

## CONISTON HALL    SD 303964

The hall-block was built by the Flemings in the 16th century and has a kitchen cross-wing on the west side and a ruined square tower wing projecting from the NE corner, with a spiral stair in the angle between it and the hall. There are said to be footings of a possible large and massive older tower just north of the west wing. Latterly the building has been partly used as a farm and partly by a sailing club.

## CORBY CASTLE    NY 470541

Corby was sold to Lord William Howard in 1625 and his son Sir William added a three storey range to a tower built by Richard de Salkeld after he was granted the manor in 1323. The tower measures 11.7m by 7.3m over walls up to 1.4m thick and has a spiral stair in the NE corner. There are brick walls and arches under the original basement vault. The new range has late 17th century pedimented windows towards the eastern approach but more irregular fenestration on the west towards the Eden. In 1812-17 Henry Howard had the tower mostly rebuilt and the space between it and the range filled in to make a rectangle, Peter Nicholson being the architect. The front is thus all 19th century with Doric columns. The interior features include a staircase and panelling and ceilings probably of the 1730s, although no work then is recorded.

*Corby Castle*

Crew Castle

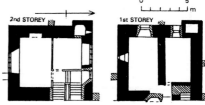

Plans of Cowmire Hall

Cowmire Hall

## COWMIRE HALL    SD 427888

Projecting from the rear or west side of a three storey house built by Richard Fleming in the 1690s is a 16th century tower built by the Briggs family. The tower measures 9.1m by 7.9m over walls about 1.2m thick. The basement contains two barrel-vaulted rooms and has remains of a rather altered zig-zag entrance passage in the east wall. Originally there seems to have been a spiral stair in the NE corner but this has been replaced by a scale-and-platt stair serving both the tower upper rooms and the main house. There are windows of three and four round-arched lights in the north and south walls at second and third storey levels, and latrines were formed in a slight projection from the north end of the west wall, which contains fireplaces. The gabled roof is a later alteration.

## CREW CASTLE    NY 568778

Only the basement remains of this building, which was the home of Will Noble in 1583. It measures 11.3m by 8.2m over walls 1.5m thick. There is a blocked doorway in the much broken down NW wall. There is another doorway in the SE wall. This side, now facing sheep-pens, and the SW end wall now obscured by a shed contain crudely formed gunloops with a pierced slab placed midway in the wall thickness with splays both in and out, the openings being covered by slabs. These features suggest a tower-like building, although since there is no vault or staircase Crew is now usually referred to as a bastle. Henry Gibson occupied "Crewhead" in 1630.

## CROGLIN RECTORY    NY 575472

A thinly-walled tower-like wing 8.6m by 5.2m with a spiral stair in the north corner and a segmental-shaped basement vault forms a cross-wing to an earlier hall on the NW later remodelled with Georgian features. Low Hall to the SW incorporates what looks like a 16th century stronghouse. A tower is referred to in an inventry of Sir Christopher Dacre when furnishings were transferred to his "house of Crogling".

## CROSBY RAVENSWORTH HALL    NY 620148

In 1286 John le Frauncey and Robert de Appleby killed Nicholas de Hastings in the ditch outside the gate. A plan of 1739 suggests the house had a double wet moat, now mostly filled in. In 1304 it was held by Henry de Threlkeld. A detached 14th century solar tower on which the Pickering family mounted their arms during remodelling c1550 was demolished in 1750. The house was purchased by Sir John Lowther and repaired by his son-in-law in 1682. Most of it has been demolished.

## DACRE CASTLE    NY 461265    V

This 14th century tower house at the east end of a moated platform has a plan which is unique in England, although there are later buildings vaguely like it in Scotland. A licence for the castle chapel was granted to Margaret de Dacre in 1354. The tower was probably then newly built, perhaps replacing or incorporating an earlier building which William de Dacre was licensed to crenellate in 1307 but destroyed by the Scots in 1317. It consists of a main block 14.3m long by 10.2m wide over walls up to 2.6m thick. Projecting diagonally from the SE corner is a turret 3m wide containing a latrine at second storey level, and a similar turret projecting from the NW corner contains small rooms on the upper two storeys. The NE corner was intended to have a third turret of this type but now has a tower 5.2m square containing several upper bedrooms but apparently solid below. The SW corner has a tower 6m by 5.2m with a spiral stair linking all three storeys and the original only entrance at its base.

The basement contains two vaulted cellars with loops facing west. The doorway between the cellars may be a later insertion since the south cellar is reached from the foot of the spiral stair and the north cellar has access via a service stair up to the main entrance passage on the east side at hall level. The outside steps leading up to this entrance are modern. The hall has a fireplace with an oven and a mural chamber in the west wall, a window and recess to the north, and on the east side a narrow loop and a lavabo with a trefoil-pointed arch and a twelve-petalled drain. The second and third storeys were given tall mullion-and-transom windows in the 1670s when after a long period of decay the tower was made habitable by Thomas Lennard, Lord Dacre, later created Earl of Sussex. His arms appear over the entrance. The castle was neglected after being purchased by Sir Christopher Musgrave in 1716 and an engraving of 1739 shows vegetation growing from the top. It was used as a farmhouse after being purchased by the Halls of Dalemain in the late 18th century. The upper parts were considered dangerous in 1923 but were restored in 1961 and the building remains occupied as a private residence.

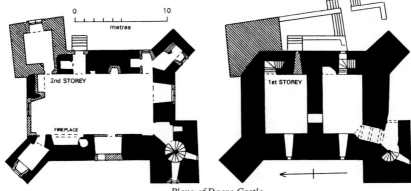

*Plans of Dacre Castle*

*Dacre Castle*

# DALLAM TOWER    SD 491810

The de Thweng family are thought to have built a tower here in the 1370s. The de Haverbracks added a hall block and the tower was replaced by another range by William Thornburgh in the 16th century. The present house was built by Daniel Wilson c1720 but contains 17th century woodwork and has a porch added in 1826.

*Dalston Hall*

*Dalton Tower*

0 — 10 metres

*Dalton Tower: plan*

1st STOREY

## DALSTON HALL    NY 377516    H

The facade facing the approach is mostly of 1899 to a design by C.J.Ferguson but towards the garden can be seen an embattled three storey tower house. It measures 8.5m by 7m over walls 1.5m thick. The thicker SE end wall contains the entrance closed by an original yett. From it is reached a spiral stair in the east corner surmounted by a turret. There are coats of arms on the turret and below the battlements is an inscription relating "Iohn Dalston Elisabet mi wyf mad ys byldyng" and a dog and cat. This indicates a date c1500. A wing adjoining it with mullioned windows and water spouts like decorated gun-barrels is 17th century.

## DALTON TOWER    SD 225739    O

Near the church on the west side of the town of Dalton-in-Furness stands a 13m high tower measuring 13.7m by 9.1m over walls from 1.5 to 1.8m thick. The north end of the west wall is thickened to 2.7m and contains a passage and a doorway onto a spiral staircase serving all the levels. There is another doorway in the south wall. The original internal layout is hard to decipher since there have been so many alterations. Originally there was a crosswall just south of the stair. The tower is thought to have been built by Furness Abbey to house a steward soon after the Scottish raids of 1314 and 1316 and to be on or near the site of a prison and courthouse mentioned in 1257. It passed to the Crown in 1539 and in 1545 it was reported that the roof leaked through lack of thatching resulting in the floors all being rotten and the lime in the walls mostly washed out. It was repaired the next year with materials from the abbey. Charles II granted the tower to the Duke of Albermarle in 1662 and it passed to the Dukes of Buccleuch, for whom considerable alterations were made. The tower served as a gaol until the 1770s and by the late 19th century was an armoury for local volunteers. In 1856 the top storeys were thrown into one.

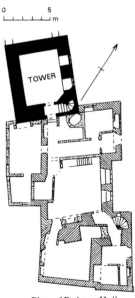

*Plan of Dalston Hall*

*Dalston Hall*

## DENTON HALL    NY 579630

Incorporated in a farmhouse of 1829 is a tower 8.9m by 8.2m over walls 1.8m thick. There is a spiral stair in the SE corner. The entrance beside it no longer goes through to the basement but still has a doorway with a shouldered lintel onto the foot of the staircase. This tower may be the "Turris de Denton juxta Hawtwisill" mentioned in the 1415 list of castles and fortalices in Northumberland. Originally there was a Denton family but the tower was held by Christopher Elwood in 1563 and by Launcelot Carleton in 1598. There are signs of surrounding earthworks.

## DOVENBY HALL    NY 094334

At the back of a Georgian house and also buried within it is a tower house with a tunnel-vaulted basement. It measures 9.2m by 6.9m over walls 1.6m thick. The NE corner is thickened to contain a mural chamber at ground level. Towards the staircase of the Georgian house probably built by Richard Lamplugh of Ribton the tower has a round-headed loop with two chamfers. If Norman as claimed it may be reset. In fact the loop is more likely to be late 14th or 15th century work, the period of the tower.

## DOWNHALL CASTLE    NY 282525

Hugh de Morville is claimed to have had a castle here but the "capital messuage" mentioned in 1232 was abandoned after being burnt by the Scots. Excavations before the site was partly levelled in 1972 found large amounts of burnt timber and part of a drawbridge was revealed 1826 when excavating farmbuilding foundations. A bank 1m high enclosed a platform 55m by 43m with a ditch. An oval second enclosure to the east 58m by 29m had a bank but no ditch. Further north is a 180m long section of wet moat 22m wide which may have once surrounded the site.

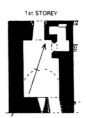

1st STOREY

*Dovenby: plan*

0                5
⌐┴┴┴┴┴┴┐m

*Drumburgh Castle*

1st STOREY

*Denton Hall: plan*

## DRAWDYKES CASTLE    NY 418586

In 1676 John Aglionby remodelled or perhaps entirely rebuilt a medieval tower house measuring about 11m by 7m. This was perhaps the "house at Triby" to which William Aglionby was unable to go in 1396 because of threats by malefactors. The house is first called Drawdykes in 1580. The present facade has three bays and three storeys with windows with pediments alternatingly segmental and triangular.

## DRUMBURGH CASTLE    NY 268598    V

The present rectangular block 22.9m long by 8.2m over walls 1.2m thick was built c1500-25 by Thomas, Lord Dacre, his arms being placed over an entrance at second storey level. The stone once had the date 1518 and was originally above the doorway below this present entrance. The basement is the remodelled lower storey of a hall-house which Robert le Brun was licensed to crenellate in 1307. It decayed after passing by marriage to Jacob Harington in the early 15th century, and was ruinous by the 1480s. Leland c1540 describes Drumburgh as "a pretty pyle for defens of the contery". In 1580 the building needed "urgent repairs" and in 1593 it was "neither castle nor tower but a house of strength occupied by a bailiff. In 1646 Cuthbert Orfeur, claiming that he had long been a tenant of the Earl of Arundel here, asked for the house to be restored to him, since he had been "violently ousted" by John Hodgson, agent to Lord Dacre. Henry, Duke of Norfolk sold the ruinous house to John Aglionby in 1678. Sir John Lowther obtained it by exchange in 1696 and made various alterations. In the 1970s it was restored after a long period of decay, the east end being carefully but entirely rebuilt, and it is now a private residence.

*Egremont Castle*

*Gatehouse, Egremont*

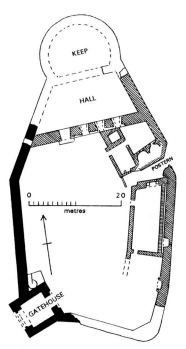

*Plan of Egremont Castle*

# EGREMONT CASTLE   NY 011102   F

In 1093 William granted most of Cumberland to Ranulf le Meschin, and his brother William is thought to have built a castle on the high natural mound here c1120. It passed by marriage to Robert de Romilli of Skipton and withstood a Scottish attack in 1138. Not long after this Egremont passed by marriage to William FitzDuncan, nephew of David I of Scotland. Later it passed to Reginald de Lucy, who died c1199, and then c1215 went to Lambert de Multon, who built the hall block before his death in 1246. The castle was probably damaged by Scottish attacks in 1315 and 1322 and in 1335 passed by marriage to Robert Fitz-Walter. He probably had little use for a castle so remote from his home in Essex and it is doubtful if it saw much future use except as a storehouse and refuge for locals. In 1371 the castle was mortgaged to raise the £1,000 ransom needed to release Walter FitzWalter, then a prisoner in Gascony. Egremont passed by marriage in the 1440s to John Radcliffe. His grandson Robert was created Earl of Sussex in 1529 and that same year sold the castle to Henry, 15th Earl of Northumberland. The castle was held by the Crown from 1537 until returned to the 16th earl in 1558. By 1578 it was very decayed and only one room was habitable. In 1682 the estate went to the Dukes of Somerset, and then in 1750 passed by marriage to the Wyndhams, Earls of Egremont. The earldom is extinct but a junior branch created Lords Leconfield and Egremont still own the site.

The castle consists of a motte rising 5m high above a bailey to the south and 12m above a surrounding platform which seems to have formed an outer court with an outer bank on the NW, and its own ditch 8m wide and 3m deep on the east. On the west a ditch 8m wide and 3m deep divides the platform from the bailey. The wall 1.8m thick on the western or more vulnerable side of the bailey has herringbone masonry, suggesting it may predate the siege of 1138. The gatehouse in the SW corner could also be of c1120-35, although it may have been refaced. It is a square of 8.2m with walls 1.6m thick and had a vault over the passage. A stair in a projection beside the curtain led to an upper room. The 13th century curtain walls on the east and south sides of the bailey are 2.1m thick. Not much of them stands above the the court, which measures 40m long by 30m wide. A fireplace near the SE corner is original. Further north is a postern reached by a passage between two late 13th or early 14th century buildings, one a bakehouse with ovens and the other probably a kitchen with two fireplaces, one inserted in the curtain wall. A new wall blocked off this fireplace when the building was remodelled as a court house.

The motte bears footings of the northern part of a late 12th century shell keep with a wall about 2m thick around a court 15m across. Much more of this keep survived until the mid 19th century. The southern part was removed in the 1220s or 30s to make room for a hall-block built out over the motte slope. The outer wall still stands high with an entrance with a draw-bar slot and holes for a pair of two light windows, plus the jamb of a third. A dog-tooth frieze ran across the front of the building going up over each window. The hall block was 13m wide externally and on the south side was 28m long. The inner wall, of which little remains, was 19m long so the block had a peculiar shape, the end walls being apparently raised on the curtains converging on the shell keep.

## EWANRIGG HALL    NY 044353

The "Law", "Myddle", and "Heigh" towers whose furnishings are listed in an inventory of "Anthony Thwaythes of Unerigg" in 1585 were probably the three storeys of the former tower about 10.7m by 9.2m over walls 1.6m thick. In 1684 Ewan Christian remodelled the tower and added a west wing, and considerable further extensions were added in 1777. The old parts were demolished in 1903.

*Hall block at Egremont*

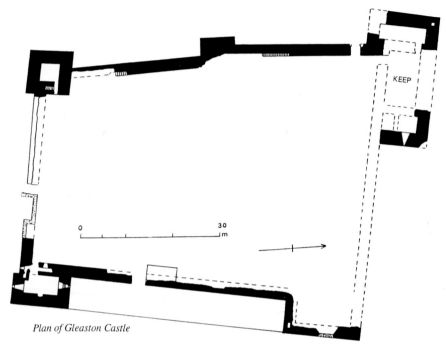

*Plan of Gleaston Castle*

## GLEASTON CASTLE   SD 261714   V

This is a rather strange building begun probably c1325 by John de Harrington, Lord of Muchland and Aldingham. It was probably left incomplete and was abandoned after the death of Sir William Harrington in 1458. Under the new owners, the Greys, it quickly decayed. Leland describes it c1540 as "the ruin and walls of the castle". Walter Curwen, bailiff to Henry Grey, 3rd Marquis of Dorset, leased and then purchased the site. Either he or his successor Thomas Preston seems to have made one of the southern towers habitable. A Richard Gaitskell was living at the castle c1639 and there may have been an occupant until the 1690s. In 1727 the Buck brothers depicted the site much as it is now. The ruin later passed to the Cavendish family but was sold to the local farmer during the first World War.

The castle consists of a curtain wall up to 2.5m thick around an irregularly shaped quadrangular court 71m long by 47m wide at the north end and 39m wide at the south end. Nothing remains of the north curtain wall and it is possible it was never completed. Only the wall faces seem to have had mortar, the core stones being set in clay. A gap on the east side may mark the entrance and there is a postern near the north end of the west wall, which has a solid tower about 9m wide projecting from the middle. The largest and most important tower lay at the NW corner of the site, the ground there being 9m higher than it is at the south end of the court. This keep is very ruined but enough remains to show it was 28m long from east to west, most of it being 12.7m wide, except that the west end projected another 3.2m to the south outside of the west curtain wall. The building seems to have contained a hall with chambers at each end over cellars. The lowest storey of the east end was further subdivided. There were latrines serving the chambers in the northern corners and at the NW corner there was a latrine at third storey level also. The upper chambers were reached by stairs against the north wall of the central room.

Little remains of the NE tower which was 17m long by 9m wide, the only surviving feature being the shute of an upper storey latrine at the SE corner. South of here the curtain is 3m high externally but almost level with the court internally. The southern towers are much better preserved, although little remains of the curtain between them. The SW tower is 12.7m high to the battlements. Higher up this tower is roughly a square of 9.6m but lower down it is more irregularly set out. It contains an unlit basement, possibly a prison, and three upper rooms, each bigger than that below because of offsets to carry the floors and having latrines in the south wall. A stair from an entrance passage through to the basement leads up in the east wall to the room above, which has a fireplace and two windows. The third storey room was reached by stairs against the west curtain, which here externally stands 9m high to wall-walk level, but without the parapet. A spiral stair in the NW corner leads to the top room and the battlements. The SW tower stands 8.7m high to the top of the parapet and contains just two storeys, both with latrines in the SW corner. The tower measures 12.9m from north to south by 9.3m wide and is entered from the court by a doorway with a pointed head and a drawbar slot. The lower room has a window at each end and a fireplace in the east wall. A stair in the west wall leads to the upper room which has four windows and a fireplace, plus a stair up to the battlements in the NW corner. Over the stair a turret rises another 3.6m. The windows in both towers are narrow pointed-headed single lights recalling the windows of 15th and 16th century tower houses in Ireland.

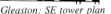

Gleaston: SE tower plan

SW tower: plan

Gleaston Castle: SE tower

Keep, Gleaston Castle

*Great Asby Rectory*

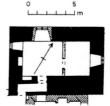

*Great Asby Rectory: plan*

*Gleaston Castle: SE tower*

## GODMOND HALL    SD 499978    V

At the east end of a late 17th century house lies a 15th century tower measuring 6.2m by 5.6m over walls up to 1.2m thick. Over a vaulted basement there are two levels, the topmost being within a later gabled roof with its axis across the width of the tower rather than lengthways.

## GREAT ASBY RECTORY    NY 680131

This building lies just south of the church and comprises a 14th century tower now of two storeys but originally possibly of three and a much altered 17th century block on the site of a former hall block whose roof mark can still be seen on the tower. The tower measures 10.2m by 7.2m over walls 1.5m thick except that the south wall is 2m thick. This wall contains a dog-leg entrance passage at its west end. The tower has one original east window with reticulated tracery and several mullioned windows of the 17th century. A wooden lock has the date 1670 and the initials A.P. for Anne Clifford, Countess of Pembroke, so the later block may be her work.

*Gleaston Castle*

*Greystoke Castle*

# GREYSTOKE CASTLE    NY 435309

In 1353 William, Lord Greystoke was licensed by Edward III to crenellate a tower here. Lying at the north end, it measured about 13m by 11m and had a wing containing tiny rooms projecting from the west end wall. Most of it was demolished during alterations of 1789 by the 16th Duke of Norfolk. He added a fourth storey to a second tower projecting diagonally from the SE corner of a walled court with a ditch on the north and west sides and steep natural slopes on the other sides. This tower measures 12m by 10.7m. The long walls are 1.5m thick and end walls are 2.4m thick to carry the thrust of a tunnel vault with five broad and flat transverse arches over a cellar with a loop at each end. The castle passed to the Grimthorpes and then from c1506 until 1569 was held by the Dacres of Naworth. The Dukes of Norfolk are descendants of Philip Howard, Earl of Arundel, who acquired it before his death in 1595. Henry Charles Howard added a wing with a fine facade in the 1670s after the castle had been a ruin since being captured in 1648 from a Royalist garrison and burnt. The neo-Elizabethan facade facing the approach was erected in 1839-48 to a design by Salvin, and he did further work at the castle after a fire in 1868.

0        20
metres

*Greystoke: plan*

*Godmund Hall*

## HARBYBROW TOWER    NY 194414

The tower house was built by the Highmore family in the mid 15th century and has several windows of that period with pairs of cusped lights. It measures 10.8m by 8.8m over walls 1.5m thick above the segmental shaped basement vault. The basement has original loops facing south and east, an inserted doorway facing north, and an original doorway in the west wall. Beside the latter is a spiral stair in the SW corner. This rises to three upper storeys and the wall-walk 11.2m above ground, now covered with flagstones. Only a partly remodelled stump remains of the parapet. The second and third storey rooms are fine chambers with big windows facing north and east and smaller windows facing south, and there are latrines in the SE corner. The third storey has a fireplace in the east wall. The fourth storey has a loop in each wall but no facilities so it must have been for servants or storage. The second storey has a fireplace in the west wall and beside it a blocked doorway which led through from a hall block on the site of the present house. An inscription of 1594 on the house is now lost but another survives from Edward VI's reign referring to 1550 when the prices of wheat, barley and malt were exceptional.

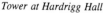
*Tower at Hardrigg Hall*                    *Harbybrow Tower*

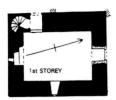

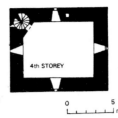
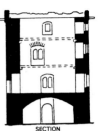

*Plans of Harbybrow Tower*

SECTION

# HARDRIGG HALL   NY 425362

Adjoining a house is one complete wall and stumps of two others of a tower 8.5m square over walls 1.4m thick. One corner contains a staircase with doorways to the second and third storeys which have fireplaces. The basement was vaulted. The top of the parapet, now destroyed, was about 9m above the ground. The tower was built by the Southaik family in the late 14th or early 15th century.

*Hardrigg: plan*

# HARTLEY CASTLE   NY 786082

The present late 18th century and early 19th century house lies in the former outer court of which traces of walls remain together with one segmental-vaulted cellar, and a mask corbel built into a garden wall. On the forfeiture of Sir Andrew Harcla in 1323, Hartley went to Ralph Neville of Raby. He sold the manor to Thomas de Musgrave who in 1353 was licensed by Edward III to crenellate his house here because it was "situated near the Scottish March and has frequently in the past been burnt and destroyed by our enemies the Scots". Richard de Musgrave, who died in 1615 added two wings, and in 1671 it was said to be "a stately house and seat, which hath received many additions by its present owner". It was later abandoned and materials taken off to repair a house at Edenhall, so that by 1773 there was "scarcely a wreck left of the castle". A sketch made in 1692 shows an inner court with ranges of three and four storey buildings and an outer court with a thick and high curtain wall, so it was clearly once an impressive building.

*Hayton Castle*

*Hayes Castle*

## HAYES CASTLE   NY 003227   V

Of a stone walled court about 22m square all that remains is about half of the north curtain wall 1.4m thick and 4.5m high. The court lay on a platform 34m square surrounded by a moat 1.5m deep and 6m wide. In 1322 Robert de Leyburn, keeper of Egremont Castle was licensed to crenellate "his dwelling house at Aykhurst". In 1374 on the death of Margaret, widow of Hugh de Moresby, it is mentioned as the "forcelet of Aykerist". The name Hayes was first used in 1600 but the castle was totally ruined by then, as it was abandoned by Christopher de Moresby, being described on his death in 1392 as "a greatly ruined castle". Two years previously malefactors broke into the buildings. In 1794 there was "a gloomy old tower on an artificial mount surrounded by an outward or curtain wall, supported by many heavy buttresses. By 1816 it was reduced to its present condition except some visible foundations and the curtain NW corner which was demolished by the farmer in 1933.

## HAYTON CASTLE   NY 110417

Hayton passed from the Tilliols to the Colvilles c1420 and by the time William Colville died in 1479 there stood on the promontory a stone house incorporating a tower. Hayton then went to the Musgraves and in 1568 Mary, Queen of Scots spent a night in the castle. There is a plaque of 1609 on the stairs and the mullioned windows of the northern end of the west front may be of that date, and perhaps also parts of the east side. The building was badly damaged during an attack by Parliamentary troops in 1648 and is said to have been much altered and repaired in the 1660s by Sir Richard Musgrave, although the windows of the southern part of the west front would go better with the date 1709 which appears on a top window, or could be still later. Sir Richard is said to have moved the entrance from the east side to the west and during this period the rest of the east side was filled in to make a building two rooms deep throughout, 27m long by 15m wide. In 1794 the house was described as "much neglected". The heavy buttresses on the east were added whilst it was in use as a farmhouse. The building has since been restored and is a private residence.

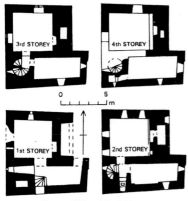

*Plans of Hazelslack Tower*

*Hollin Hall*

*Hazelslack Tower*

## HAYTON MOTTE NY 507578

On the north side of the village is a narrow scarped ridge up to 24m high with an overgrown and damaged ringwork 19m across with a rampart 1m high above the interior. The castle was perhaps built by the de Vaux family, granted Hayton by Henry II.

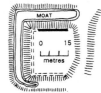

*Hayes Castle; plan*

## HAZELSLACK TOWER SD 477788

This ruined 14th century building beside a farmyard served as a solar block to a hall block of which the only relic is a 3.8m wide kitchen fireplace on the lower of two storeys. The east wall of the northern part of the block is over 2m thick to accommodate the fireplace and its flue, but the other walls are just 0.9m thick. The north part contains rooms about 4m square, the lowest level having had a segmental-shaped vault. The three upper levels have fireplaces in the east wall and the third and fourth storeys had mullioned windows to the north and west. The south part of the building projects further east and contains four levels of unvaulted rooms up to 2.2m wide and 5m long. In the SW corner is a spiral stair rising from the second storey to the top of the building. Latrines are squeezed in beside it at the second and fourth storey levels.

*Hazelslack Tower*

## HIGHHEAD CASTLE    NY 403433

The first mention of a tower at "Heyheved" is in 1323 concerning its garrison. It was granted in 1327 to William L'Engleys, Chief Forester of Inglewood and he decided to rebuild it because it was decayed and its foundations were inadequate, being licensed in 1342 by Edward III to crenellate his manor house here. It is first described as a castle in 1357. In the 1370s the castle passed by marriage to the Restwold family. They sold it in 1542 to John Richmond whose descendants lived here until it passed by marriage to Henry Richmond Brougham c1739. A print of about that time shows a domestic range standing on the west side of a neglected rectangular court with a crenellated parapet and vegetation growing on the wall-walk, plus a three storey gatehouse on the north side with diagonal buttresses and a SE stair turret. In 1744-8 the new owner replaced the courtyard with a new mansion with a classical facade. Before the internal features were complete the house passed to co-heirs, neither of them able to occupy it because of legal difficulties, although the mid 16th century range 15.8m long at the west end with windows with arched lights remained occupied by a farmer. One of the co-heirs began demolition of his half in the 1770s but before much was removed the first Lord Broughton purchased the house. Some work was done on it after the Hill family purchased the mansion in 1902. A fire in 1956 gutted the 18th century part but the 16th century wing is still habitable. Projecting from its SW corner in an awkward manner is a later wing 7.3m by 5.5m. To the NW is a late 18th century stable-block. The house has a fine defensive site with steep drops on the east, south and west to a loop of the River Ive.

## HOLLIN HALL    SD 466961

The central part of this two-storey house of the Philipson family, later held by the Flemings, is late 16th century and the west wing is 17th or early 18th century. At the east end and on a different alignment is a tower just 7.2m long by 5.5m wide. The vaulted basement is entered through a doorway broken through the 0.9m thick south end wall. Rather thicker are the north wall containing a fireplace and loop and the west wall containing the blocked original entrance, off which leads a spiral stair in the NW corner. The stair leads to a thinly walled upper room with narrow loops and a fireplace and latrine in the thick north end wall. Above are crow-stepped gables.

*Howgill Castle*

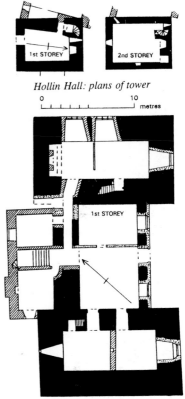

Hollin Hall: plans of tower

Plan of Howgill Castle

Highhead Castle

# HOWGILL CASTLE   NY 669292

John de Lancaster built this interesting house, described as a castle in his will dated 1354. In the 1430s it passed to the Crackanthorpes and then later to the Sandford family. It consists of a pair of cross-wings each about 15.6m long by 9m wide with walls up to 2.6m thick lying at either end of a hall 6.2m wide by 11m long. The hall SE wall is only 1m thick but the NW wall is as thick as those of the wings and contains a passage and remains of a staircase above which are stepped trefoiled arches. A wing containing rooms and a scale-and-platt staircase was added on that side in the 17th century. The cross-wings have cellars with segmental vaults and straight staircases leading up in the walls adjoining the hall. Each contains several 16th century windows, and there are 17th century windows in the NE wall of the NE wing. The SW wing contained the pantry and buttery each reached by doorways from the hall. The basement in the NE wing may have originally only been reached from the solar above. The castle was garrisoned for King Charles by Sir Richard Sandford who purchased twenty muskets for the defenders. It passed by marriage in 1723 to the Honeywoods and in 1733 the parapets on the wings were mostly removed, the hall block raised up to the same height of three storeys and new windows and a central dooirway provided on the SE side. On the NW side the parapets of the wings are incorporated in low gables. The Honeywoods sold Howgill to the Tuftons c1780 and the castle was used as a farmhouse until 1851 and then allowed to decay. It was restored from a derelict condition in 1967 and is still inhabited.

*Hutton John: plan*

*Hutton-in-the-Forest*

# HUTTON-IN-THE-FOREST   NY 460358

Thomas de Hoton, who died in 1362, probably built the tower measuring 11.4m by 8.4m over walls 1.9m thick. It has a vaulted basement and a spiral stair in the east corner. South of it is a much-altered hall-range, beyond which is the south tower, a Victorian structure standing above a medieval vaulted basement of greater extent. In 1606 the house was sold to the Fletchers, rich merchants of Cockermouth. Sir Henry Fletcher added a long gallery east of the tower house in the 1640s. It has an open arcade below it and a central canted bay on the south. Sir George Fletcher c1680 added the central facade of the hall block in a Baroque style and a fine new staircase.

# HUTTON JOHN   NY 440270

At the SE corner is a tower house measuring 11m by 8.6m over walls 1.5m thick, but they are thickened to contain an entrance lobby on the north side with a spiral stair in the adjacent NW corner. The basement has a small fireplace with a smoke-hole in the wall. The upper storeys both have latrines and small sleeping chambers in the wall thickness. These levels now have sash windows. A hall-range west of the tower was given a third storey and new windows in 1830. The range north of the tower was added by Andrew Hudleston and is dated 1662. It has mullion-and-transom windows on the upper levels and heart-shaped windows below, apparently an oblique reference to Huddleston's catholicism, since one other heart high up at the north end has a cross. This wing has a doorway with the date 1739 on the door-lock and a ceiling and staircase also of that period. The entrance hall and library added in 1866 were designed by George Ledwall Taylor, related by marriage to the Hudlestons, who still own the property. The original house was at a moated site 145m to the east.

# IRTHINGTON CASTLE   NY 499614

The motte east of the church was probably built in the 1160s by Hubert de Vaux or his son Robert. Until lowered in the early 19th century this mound rose 9m above a ditch 9m wide to a summit 23m across. There is said to have been a bailey to the SE but the farm on the west side supposedly lies on the site of a court 29m by 22m with a tower at the south corner of the curtain wall. This would have been the work of the de Multons, who obtained the barony by marriage c1240. It passed to the Dacres c1317. Their castle at Naworth was improved in the 17th century by the Howards supposedly using materials from the ruined castles of Irthington and Kirkoswald.

## IRTON HALL    NY 105005

The neo-Elizabethan house built for J.L.Burns Lindow in 1874 to a design by Grayson and now used as flats incorporates a well preserved tower house with a vaulted basement and one mutilated window with twin lancets. It measures 9.7m by 6.4m over walls 1.8m thick and has a spiral stair in the SW corner.

## ISEL HALL    NY 158337

This four storey 15th century tower by the River Derwent retains several original mullioned windows and measures 11.8m by 7.1m and rises 12.5m high to the top of the embattled parapet. A straight stair rises between the main vaulted basement and a smaller vault filling most of the south end, with the entrance passage east of it. South of the tower is a 16th century hall-block with two fireplaces, one near the dais and another backing onto the screens passage with original linenfold panelling. This range was later extended to the west and now has three storeys with fairly regularly spaced three-light windows on the upper levels. Further extensions to the west and east are 18th and 19th century respectively. Isel belonged to the de Multons, then the Leighs and Lawsons whose arms appear on the later extensions.

## JOHNBY HALL    NY 434328

A wing at the east end of the south front contains a wide spiral stair at the top of which is an umbrella-vault. Opening onto this stair is a doorway with an elaborately framed inscription referring to William Musgrave and Isabel Martendale and the date 1583. The framing and the plan of the hall are more akin to contemporary buildings in Scotland than England. A passage leads from the entrance past two vaulted cellars, one of which has a service stair, to a kitchen at the west end with a fireplace formed in a projection from the north wall. This part has thicker walling and may incorporate a medieval tower of the Johnby family measuring about 9.7m by 8m. The hall was improved in the 1650s by Sir Edward Musgrave but was later leased to the Williams family, who built a stable and coach house to the south. The hall passed to the Hasells in 1696, was sold to the 10th Duke of Norfolk in 1783 and was modernised by Mrs Leyburn Popham, a tenant, in the early 20th century.

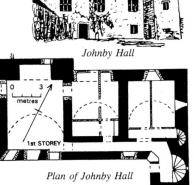

*Johnby Hall*

*Plan of Johnby Hall*

*Johnby Hall*

*Johnby: the ornate entrance*

*Castle Howe motte, Kendal*

# KENDAL CASTLE   SD 512923 & 522925

The original castle of Kendal was probably the motte and bailey on Castle Howe at the east end of a ridge west of the town. The bailey 80m long by 60m wide has been built over but the motte survives, rising 15m to a summit 18m across. This earthwork probably goes back the time of either Ivo de Taillebois, granted the barony c1087, or Ketel, granted the barony by Henry I. It was probably Ketel's grandson William, who assumed the name de Lancaster, that transferred his seat to the ringwork on Castle Hill east of the town. The curtain wall is thought to be the work of Gilbert Fitz Reinfred, who obtained Kendal by marriage c1184 and lived until 1220. It was confiscated by King John in 1215 but restored by Henry III to Gilbert's son William. In 1246 Kendal passed to Peter de Brus and in c1272 passed by marriage to the de Roos family. In 1383 Sir William Parr obtained Kendal by marrying Elizabeth de Roos.

Catherine Parr was the the daughter of Sir Thomas who died in 1518 when she was very young. Despite other claims she was actually born in Northamptonshire. She became the sixth and last wife of Henry VIII in 1542, having already been widowed twice. After Henry died in 1547 Catherine married Sir Thomas Seymour, brother of Henry's third wife Jane, and uncle to the young Edward VI, and she eventually died in childbirth. In 1553 Queen Mary confiscated Kendal from William Parr, Marquis of Northampton, but Elizabeth I returned it in 1559. After he died in 1571 it passed by exchange to the Crown. A survey in 1572 records" The out walls embattled 40 foot square - within the same no building left, saving only in the north side is situate the front of the gatehouse. The hall with an ascent of the stairs to the same, with a buttery and pantry at the end therof, one great chamber and 2 or 3 lesser chambers, and rooms of ease, adjoining the same, all being in decay both in glass and slates and in all other repairs needful. Under the hall are two or three small rows of cellars. In the south side is situated a dove-cot. The walls are circular, guarded by three towers and a keep, with a large square area in the centre, all being in a state of delapidation. In its doors and window jambs, and in a few quoins we find the red sandstone, but the main work is built with unhewn blue rock from the hills". The ruin was acquired by the Fanes, Earls of Westmorland, but was sold c1667 to Sir Charles Anderton. The keep and the walls and towers look ruined but almost complete on a print of 1739. Repairs were executed in 1813 and Lord Bentinck consolidated the ruin in 1896 before it was handed over to the Kendal Corporation.

*Hall block, Kendal Castle*

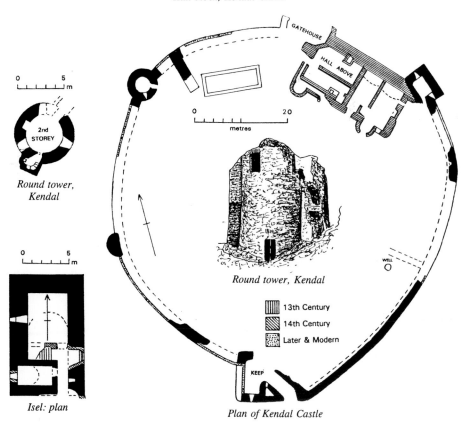

*Round tower,
Kendal*

*Isel: plan*

*Round tower, Kendal*

13th Century
14th Century
Later & Modern

*Plan of Kendal Castle*

The castle was crudely built and is now very ruined. The curtain wall is 1.8m thick and now best preserved on the south where it stands 3m above the steep slope down the side of the ringwork to the surrounding ditch and 1.2m above the internal level. On the west the wall is destroyed to courtyard level and a thin modern parapet lies on its outer edge. The courtyard is circular with a maximum diameter of 70m. Providing some measure of flanking fire on the west were a solid half-round turret 4.4m in diameter and a circular tower 6.3m in diameter containing a living room with two windows, a fireplace and its own upper doorway from the wall-walk. A projection rising up from the curtain contains a combined latrine and staircase. Below the living room is a dome-vaulted cellar with a single loop facing the court.

At the south end of the court is the keep, a rectangular tower about 11m by 10m long with rounded corners. There is a room to the west, a vault to the east and part of a semi-circular wall face of an oven or stair-well. On the NE side of the court is a rectangular tower with two offsets on the side facing the field, which is 8m long. South of this tower is a latrine shoot in the curtain wall base. The tower adjoins the remains of a 14th century block which contained a hall with two cellars below its eastern end. The hall was 9m wide and about 17m long, its NW wall being lost and the SW wall destroyed above the vaults of the cellars. From the south wall projected a polygonal stair turret and a square bay. There are windows high up in the outer wall towards the field. At this level is an upper chamber with a latrine in the adjacent tower, but this did not communicate directly with the hall.

At the NW end of the hall-block are slight traces of a gatehouse with a pair of elongated polygonal towers about 5m wide flanking a central passage. It is unfortunate that so little of it survives as the only comparable structure in the north of England is the Warkworth gatehouse. In front lay the 12m square barbican mentioned in the 1572 survey. West of the gatehouse are thin footings for a what was perhaps a timber framed chapel about 5m wide by 12.4m long although Machell's sketch shows the chapel further SE. A thick wall west of these footings may be a relic of an older hall-block lying on this site or a ramp with a stair to the curtain wall-walk rising at right-angles to the curtain.

*Keep, Kendal Castle*

Kentmere Hall

Kirkandrews: plan of tower

Plans of Kentmere Hall

Kirkandrews Tower

## KENTMERE HALL    NY 451042

The now much altered and subdivided hall and a cross-wing at the east end are 15th century, the hall-block having a 17th century roof with cambered tie-beams and collars. At the west end is a 14th century tower 9m from north to south by 6.7m wide over walls 1.5m thick. Thinner walls still stand three storeys high above the basement vault but a single lean-to roof now replaces the original upper floors and roof. At the top are remains of a corbelled parapet. A projection from the north end of the west wall contains latrines and a spiral stair is squeezed into the NE corner. The basement had loops at each end, that on the north now broken out to form an entrance. The east doorway from the hall-block is later. The second storey has an original window with trefoiled ogee-headed lights under a square head. Kentmere belonged to the Gilpin family from c1375 and was sold to the Philipsons c1660.

## KIRKANDREWS TOWER    NY 389719

The tower measures 10.1m by 7.3m over walls 1.5m thick and has a vaulted basement with an original loop at each end. The entrance lies in the south wall and a spiral stair rises from it in the SE corner. There are two upper storeys plus an attic within the step-gabled roof within a corbelled parapet rising 11.4m above the basement floor, which is slightly below ground level. The tower looks more Scottish than English and was probably built c1530-50 by Thomas Graham. The Grahams lived in the "Debateable Land", a tract of land neither definately Scottish or English, and were noted for their acts of lawlessness in both countries. They are still here. The castellated wall of the farm is 19th century. A well was discovered in 1986.

*SE tower, Kirkoswald Castle*

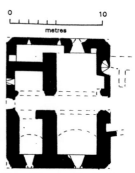

*Plan of Lammerside Castle*

# KIRKOSWALD CASTLE   NY 555409 & 559409

West of the church is a large double ditched enclosure in the middle of which is a platform 50m by 20m within a ditch up to 8m wide. The wooden tower said to have been built by Ralph Engaine may have been on this site which is overlooked by high ground beyond the church. By 1158 Kirkoswald had passed to Simon de Morville and his son Hugh was licensed to crenellate his manor house here a year before he died in 1202. It then passed to Richard de Lucy of Egremont and then c1213 to the de Multons. Thomas de Multon III and his widow's second husband John de Castre both made additions to the house but it is said to have been burnt by the Scots in 1314.

In 1317 Ranulph, Lord Dacre, obtained Kirkoswald by abducting the heiress Margaret de Multon from Warwick Castle and marrying her. It is probable that the second site SE of the village was then laid out with substantial stone buildings. There is mention of "a castle newly built" on the death of Humphrey, Lord Dacre in 1485, but it seems that he just altered a castle of c1330-50. Thomas, Lord Dacre, who died in 1525, "did finish and moat about with great charge" the building works there. It was allowed to decay after the Dacres were forfeited for rebellion in 1569, and in the early 17th century Lord William Howard took material from the castle for alterations to his chief seat at Naworth. In one of the towers at Naworth is a fine timber ceiling of c1340-50 from Kirkoswald with moulded beams and bosses and panels with flowing tracery. By 1688 the castle was "a bare shell or heap of stones" and there was further dismantling after Sir Christopher Musgrave purchased the ruin c1715.

The castle has an overgrown enclosure 115m by 90 surrounded by a moat 2m deep and up to 12m wide. The SE corner of the enclosure is recessed and the same feature appears in the plan of the stone building lying in a very fragmentary state in the middle. Overall the castle measured about 46m each way over walls up to 2.4m thick. Lying half-buried under piles of debris are vaulted cellars in the bases of the SW tower measuring about 10.5m by 9m, and the SE tower, a square of about 9m, the walls being about 2m thick. These towers stood about 15m apart. On the north side was a hall about 18m long by 10m wide with a thick south wall which partly survives and a solar tower about 15m by 13m to the east of it from which must have come the ceiling now at Naworth. The vaulted cellar of this tower is full of rubble. Parts of the second storey adjoin the only high fragment of the castle, a latrine turret 4m wide and 20m high set diagonally at the NW corner. The fragment of the hall north wall adjoining is just 1.2m thick, thinner than other surviving walls, perhaps evidence of late 15th and early 16th century rebuilding. There may have been other diagonal projecting turrets at the eastern corners of the tower. Nothing now remains of a gateway on the west side of the court flanked by towers about 7m square.

*Lammerside Castle*

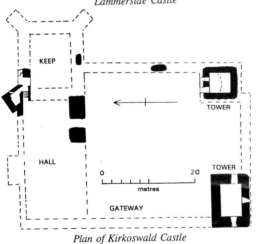

*Plan of Kirkoswald Castle*

*Kirkoswald Castle*

# LAMMERSIDE CASTLE   NY 773048   V

This 14th century building seems to have formed a solar block. There was evidently a block joining at right angles to the south and this may have contained a hall. From it a stair not connecting with any of the cellars led up. The surviving block measures 13.9m by 11.4m over walls up to 1.5m thick and now 4.5m high. A central passage divides two segmental-vaulted cellars on the south and two smaller vaulted rooms on the north. A fifth room in the NE corner seems to have contained a latrine. The arrangement recalls that of the northern cross-wing at Burneside Hall. One is tempted to suggest the northern part except the latrine is later but there is no evidence of a join, the whole of both storeys being apparently of one period. The upper level had one large chamber with a south fireplace and several windows, plus a latrine in the NE corner and two private rooms on the north side divided off by thin walls now destroyed. Little is known of the history of this enigmatic ruin. The Warcops may have erected it and the Whartons may have occupied it until the early 15th century.

*Lanercost Vicarage*

*Dacre Tower, Lanercost Priory*

## LAMPLUGH HALL    NY 088207

The farmhouse of 1821 is thought to have been built from materials from a 15th century tower shown as complete and clad with ivy on a drawing of 1778 by George Monkhouse. This also shows the detached Elizabethan house burnt down soon after and replaced by the present house. A gatehouse still survives but was mostly rebuilt after a yew fell upon it in a gale in 1961, the datestone of 1595 with arms of Sir John Lamplugh being subsequently replaced by a replica.

## LANERCOST    NY 556637    E

On the SW side of the priory is a tower 11.4m by 9.8 with windows with mullions and transoms and others with pairs of pointed lights under square heads. These match those inserted into the adjoining west range of the claustral buildings by Sir Thomas Dacre, who made that part his residence after the priory was dissolved in the 1530s. So the upper storeys, making the building into a tower, are evidently of the 1540s or 50s. The lower parts contained a kitchen with fireplaces and an oven over a basement. A stair in the NE corner led up from the kitchen. Close to the NW of the west range stands the vicarage, a thinly walled structure measuring 7.5m by 6.5m also known as King Edward's Tower, supposedly after Edward I, although it had only one storey before the 1550s and the battlements and dog-tooth frieze may be as late as the 1850s. A possible motte lies by Lanercost Bridge.

## LEVENS HALL    SD 495851    O

Much of this famous Elizabethan house was built after James Bellingham obtained Levens in the late 16th century from the de Redman family, owners since c1225. However there are medieval doorways and masonry remaining from what seems to have been a hall block with an embattled cross-wing with a still surviving tunnel vaulted basement at the west end and another cross-wing at the east end. The house was sold to James Graham in 1688 and later passed by marriage to the Howard Earls of Suffolk. In 1807 they added the Howard Tower beyond the kitchen wing of 1703 extending to the south. West of the tower is a wing of 1692.

## LIDDEL STRENGTH    NY 402742

Over the years there has been much confusion between this site and that of Liddel in Roxburghshire 19km to the NE. The Cumbrian Liddel is thought to have been erected by Turgis Brundis, who was granted the manor by Ranulph de Meschin during Henry I's reign. His son William supported the Scots and was allowed to remain in possession when they ruled Cumbria from 1136 to 1157, after which the castle and manor were granted by Henry II to Nicholas de Stuteville. The castle was captured by the Scots under William the Lion in 1174, and was briefly confiscated by the English Crown in the period 1217-1220. It passed by marriage to the Wake family c1233. On the death of Baldwin Wake in 1282 Liddel is described as a castle "containing a wooden hall, with two solars, cellars and a chapel, also a kitchen, a byre, a grange and a wooden granary which threatens ruin but might now be repaired". In 1300 Edward I ordered Simon de Lindsay, who had possession because the heir was a minor, to "repair the Mote and the fosses around it, strengthening and redressing the same and the pele and palisades, and making lodges within the mote if necessary for the safety of the men-at-arms of the garrison".

In 1342 Sir Walter Selby and his two sons were executed by David II of Scotland after the Scots besieged a garrison of two hundred men in the wooden castle, storming and burning it after four days. Thomas Wake reoccupied the site and is thought to have begun the stone tower of which footings 10m by 8m remain in the inner bailey, but it is unlikely that the castle saw much use after he died in 1349. Liddel then passed to John of Woodstock, and in 1357 was granted to John of Gaunt, Earl of Richmond, later Duke of Lancaster, merging with the Crown estates on Henry IV's accession in 1399. The "square tower of excellent masonry" noted at Leddel Strength in 1794 had vanished a century later.

The castle lies high above the steep wooden bank of the River Liddel, facing Scotland on the north bank. The inner bailey 60m by 55m has a slight bank to the north and east and a bank 11m high and a ditch 8m deep on the west and south. It was probably a ringwork to which a motte was added on the east. This mound, now damaged on its east side, rises 25m above the eastern ditch to a summit 11m across. To the west is an outer bailey 55m by 69m with a rampart and ditch, and there is an oval mound at the east end of its ditch, probably the site of the outer entrance.

Whatever buildings the absentee landlords required at Liddel in the late medieval period probably lay at the moated site of Highmoat just to the SW. The Mote of Liddel burnt by the Scots in 1528 was probably this site. The Grahams acquired it by 1553 and are said to have erected a hall and chapel, abandoned in the early 17th century.

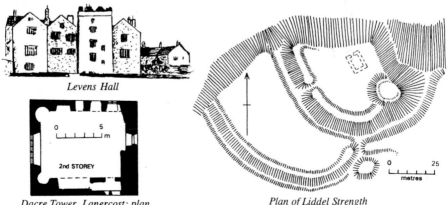

*Levens Hall*

*Dacre Tower, Lanercost: plan*

2nd STOREY

0    5    m

*Plan of Liddel Strength*

0    25    metres

## LINSTOCK CASTLE   NY 429586

At the start of Henry III's reign the Bishop of Carlisle acquired the manor and soon erected a house which was large enough to accommodate Edward I and his retinue for six days in 1307. The tower 9.6m by 8.5m over walls 2m thick may have existed by then. It has a pointed-vaulted basement and single chamfered doorways into both the first and second storeys, the upper one now blocked. The stair in the east corner connecting these levels has gone. A straight stair led from the second storey to a third storey which contained two rooms. The house adjoining the east corner has traces of 15th century work (and later mullioned windows). By 1450 the bishops ceased to use Linstock as a residence and it became a refuge and prison. Mariota Richardson paid a rent of 10s for the castle in 1461-2. By the mid 17th century it had become a farmhouse. The tower was given a new roof and windows c1768 by James Nicolson. The Church Commissioners sold the house in 1863 and it remains a private residence. There are traces of a ditch to the west and north.

## LOWTHER CASTLE   NY 522239 & 519251

The huge ruin of 1806-11 lies immediately north of the site of Lowther Hall, long the seat of the Lowther family. Sir John Lowther was made Viscount Lonsdale two years after he rebuilt the hall in 1692. Until then the building consisted of a 16th century hall remodelled in 1630 (using a roof from the hall of Kirkoswald Castle) lying between an east tower of c1350 and a later western tower. Later wings survived the rebuilding. The hall was burnt in 1718 and plundered by the Jacobites in 1745.

In the plantation of Castlesteads above the river to the north is an enclosure 28m by 22m now lacking its ditch but having at the SE a 3m high oval mound which could be a tiny motte but more probably covers the last remains of an early tower house.

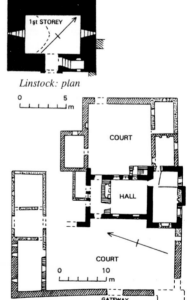

Linstock: plan

Linstock Castle

Plan of Middleton Hall

## MELMERBY HALL    NY 612373

The oldest parts of the present building appear to be late 16th century, there once being a datestone of 1597. The western extensions of 1794 probably replaced the tower thought to have been built by John de Wigton, which Edward II ordered to be safely guarded against the Scots after he died in 1315. A record probably of c1322 says "John de Denum kept a garrison of twelve men at his tower of Melmerby".

## MIDDLETON  HALL    SD 626875

The de Middletons' 14th century hall-block with north and south cross-ranges divides two courts with 15th century enclosing walls 1.4m thick. The east court measures about 14m by 15m not including the lesser ranges on its north and south sides. The eastern part of the south range is modern. The western court has an archway and windows above of a former gatehouse. This court is 15m wide and 32m long and has a 16th century stable within its northern end. The hall was 12m long by 7m wide but in the 16th century it was reduced to a square by replacing the former timber partition of the screens passage at the north end with a substantial wall containing a big fireplace, now mostly blocked. The screens passage has original doorways at each end and three which led to a pantry and buttery on either side of a passage through the north wing to a former kitchen beyond. The hall has two 15th century windows and a stair in a 16th century projection on the east side to the south wing upper rooms. The south wing has a large chimney stack on the south side, west of which are 16th century windows, the lower with round arched lights, the upper with four centred heads to the lights. East of the chimney stack is a 17th century window. By that period Middleton was held by the Askews.

*Middleton Hall*

*Millom Castle*

## MILLOM CASTLE    SD 171813    V

The motte with a ditch to the east and south on which the castle stans may go back to when Godard de Boyville was granted the manor in 1134. It passed c1240 to the de Hudlestons and in 1335 Edward III licensed John de Hudleston to crenellate his manor house at "Millum". From then remain the walls 1.8m thick on the north and east sides of a court 28m by 23m. The north side has two big window embrasures with seats which lighted a hall. The fine upper chamber 13m long by 6.5m in the SE corner is assumed to have been a solar but its position remote from the hall is unusual. This block projects south beyond the outer wall and has fireplaces on the east side. A kitchen block has replaced the NE corner of the court, its north wall projecting beyond the original outer wall, whilst its east wall is mostly within the line of the original. Between the kitchen and the solar is a small court with a gateway facing east. The roll-moulded inner gate arch must be Elizabethan but the embrasure with a drawbar slot is probably older. The outer arch (now destroyed) was reached by a flight of open steps up the mound slope. A fragment of the inner arch of an earlier gateway with a portcullis groove adjoins the kitchen block near its SW corner.

The tower house 15.2m square and 13.4m high on the west side was built either after the castle was damaged by the Lancastrians c1460 or was perhaps added by Ferdinand de Hudleston, who was given a licence to crenellate in 1522. It occupies much of the original small central court and seems to have taken over the function of the hall block, which probably then became an open space with its south wall just beyond the tower north wall being taken down. Each of the four storeys of the tower is divided by a north-south crosswall into two equal parts. The vaulted cellars were reached from the court. The upper levels are connected by a spiral stair in the NE corner and a wider scale-and-platt stair has been inserted later into the NW corner. Modern walls divide off the truncated main rooms from passages at the north end connecting the two stairs. The castle was captured and slighted by Parliamentary troops in 1644. Repairs were made in the 1670s but a Buck print of 1739 shows the building as it is now with the tower house occupied by a farmer but the rest in decay.

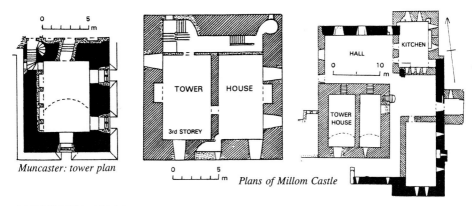

*Muncaster: tower plan*

*Plans of Millom Castle*

## MORESBY HALL   NX 984210

Facing the approach is a fine western facade of c1690-1700 with rustication and pediments which are alternately segmental and triangular. Hidden behind this range lies an older mansion with mullion-and-transom windows and three ranges set around a court originally with just a screen wall on the west. The staircase of the added west range almost fills the court. No tower is discernable, despite claims of one.

## MUNCASTER CASTLE   SD 103965

Benedict de Pennington held Muncaster by 1185. The family adopted Muncaster as their surname some time after transferring their main seat here from Pennington. Projecting from one corner of the present mansion on a spur above the Esk estuary is a tower house of the 1320s measuring 11.7m by 8.9m over walls 2.1m thick. The staircase is in the NW corner but is not connected with the entrance in the north end wall. There is also a service stair linking the lowest two levels. Some medieval walling also survives on the north side of the mansion which measures 58m by 18m and seems to replace a former open court. The tower at the NW corner was built in the 1860s by Salvin for the 4th Lord Muncaster. Most of the building is of that period but the octagonal library east of the tower house dates from an earlier building campaign of the 1780s. The castle is still occupied by the present Lord Muncaster.

*Old postcard of Muncaster Castle*

## NAWORTH CASTLE    NY 559627

The de Multons had a manor house or tower on this strong promontory site above two streams. It is thought to have been destroyed by the Scots shortly before 1317 when Ranulph de Dacre obtained the estate by abducting and marrying the heiress Margaret de Multon. Ranulph was licensed to crenellate his house here in 1335 and it was strong enough to withstand an attack by David II of Scotland in 1346. It comprised a court with a curtain wall 2.4m thick and up to 8m high with the Dacre Tower 9m square and 18m high projecting from the east end of the south wall. This side is 45m long and contains a gateway of 1844 probably on the site of the main original entrance beside the tower. The west side of the court is 33m long and the north and east sides are 52m long. The vulnerable east side contains a narrow 16th century entrance with a yett and has in front two dry ditches, the inner one now a sunk garden and the outer one set in front of a narrow later outer court flanked by the outer gatehouse and the "Boathouse". The inner wall here lacks any means of providing flanking fire but there may have originally been another square 14th century tower projecting at the north end of this side, in front of where the Howard Tower was formed in the 1530s by building arches across the sharp angle made by the curtain walls here. This was part of a remodelling by Thomas, Lord Dacre, who added a fifth storey and higher stair turret to the other tower and four new ranges of domestic buildings, with a hall 23m long by 7m wide in the north range.

In the late 1560s the estate passed to a minor who died in a house belonging to Sir Richard Palmerstone at Thetford in Norfolk when a vaulting horse collapsed on him, crushing his head. The three co-heiresses all married into the Howard family but the castle was seized by their uncle Leonard Dacre, only to be confiscated by Elizabeth I because of his part in the rebellion of 1569. With no occupant the castle decayed. In 1589 it was described as "a fair castle - of good strength and built four square with a gatehouse to the same....it is now in very great decay in all parts and the outhouses and other houses and offices are utterly decayed". It was noted that the south range (which contained a chapel) was never completed.

*Old postcard of courtyard at Naworth Castle*

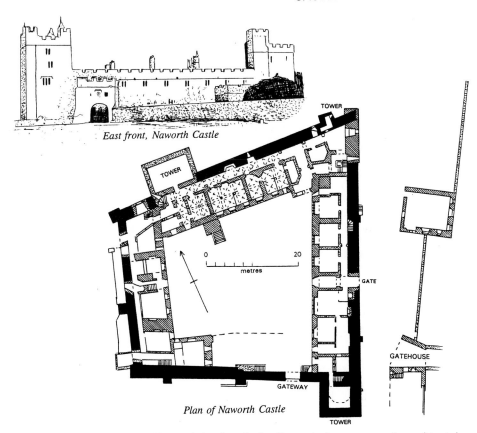

*East front, Naworth Castle*

*Plan of Naworth Castle*

In 1601 Lord William Howard, husband of a Dacre heiress, was allowed to take possession of the Dacre estate on payment to the Crown of £10,000. Considerable work was done to the buildings over the next twenty years. It was he who inserted the fine mid 14th century ceiling from Kirkoswald Castle into the the tower which bears his name. His family of 52 people including his childrens' spouses and their children all lived at the castle. The building was garrisoned for Parliament by Sir Charles Howard in the 1640s and 50s. He supported the Restoration of Charles II in 1660 and was created Earl of Carlisle the following year. From then until a fire gutted the hall block in 1844 no alterations of note seem to have been effected. Salvin was called in by George, Earl of Carlisle, to restore the building. Most of his work reproduces what was there before but the Morpeth Tower near the north end of the NE side was a new addition. The outer ward defences were then mostly removed.

## NETHERBY HALL     NY 396717

Hidden at the back of the house is a 15th century tower measuring 12.5m by 9m over walls up to 2.3m thick with a segmental-vault in the basement and a spiral stair in the SW corner. It passed to the Grahams in the 16th century and was extended. The hall and dining room has 17th century panelling, whilst some of the interior features were executed for Dr Robert Graham c1760. Some of his work may remain in the front facade but it now looks mostly the work of William Burn in the 1830s.

## NETHERHALL    NY 041366

The considerable 18th and 19th century additions were demolished in 1979 after being gutted by fire. The 14th century tower thus stands alone, but much altered and with its openings closed up. It measures 10.8m by 8.4m over walls 2.4m thick. There are original loops in the end walls and a passage and possible original entrance on the NW side. The basement is subdivided, one room having a large later fireplace. On the opposite side of the River Ellen is a rectangular moated platform, perhaps intermediate in date between the Maryport ringwork to the west and Netherhall.

## NEWBIGGIN  HALL    NY 433508

A 14th century tower house with a vaulted basement and a spiral staircase lies hidden behind a late 17th century symmetrical facade of seven bays with a central doorway with a curly open pediment. Until this facade was created by William Graham the building retained its battlements. The old part measures 17m by 9m over walls 2m thick but the more thinly walled NE end may indicate that a tower about 12.5m long was extended later. Some of the other features are early 19th century.

## NEWBIGGIN  HALL    NY 628286

The east (actually NE) tower 13.4m by 8.7m with walls 1.4m thick is thought to have been built by the Crackenthorpes after they acquired Newbiggin by marriage c1332, but was remodelled c1500. A stair turret projects from the NW end wall and beyond it is a wing known as the Jerusalem Tower added either in 1461 or c1500. The hall block adjoins both parts and is of 1533 but rebuilt in 1796 and 1844. Beyond is a west wing of 1564 remodelleed in 1844 and supposedly on the site of a large 14th century tower. On the other side of the Jerusalem Tower is a wing of 1891.

## ORMSIDE  HALL    NY 701176

This building just SE of the church (which lies on a ringwork 50m by 35m and 4 to 6m high) was built by the Bartons in the late 14th century. It passed to Sir Christopher Pickering in the late 16th century and then in the 17th century went to the Hiltons, who rebuilt the central block containing the hall and eventually added other ranges beyond on the site of a former cross wing at the NE end. The cross-wing in the form of a three storey tower at the SW end measures 11m by 8m over walls 1.4m thick. Originally there was a spiral stair in a wing projecting from the east end of the NE side with the entrance adjoining to the west of it. The SE wall has one original second storey window with two trefoiled lights under a square head, and traces of a similar window below, whilst the window above is 15th century. Another 15th century window remains above two 17th century ones in the NW wall, whilst the SW wall contains larger 17th century windows with segmental-arched lights. The second storey contains a 17th century plaster frieze with scrolls.

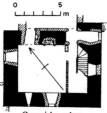

*Netherhall: plan*     *Ormside: plan*          *Newbiggin Hall*

*Pendragon Castle*

*Pendragon Castle*

# PENDRAGON CASTLE   NY 782026   V

This castle by the east bank of the River Eden consists of a tower 19.4m square over walls up to 4.4m thick with very broad clasping pilaster buttresses at the corners standing in the middle of a platform with a northern ditch 3m deep and 9m wide crossed by two causeways. It was burnt accidentally in 1541 and not restored until the Lady Anne Clifford made it habitable in 1660-1. It was dismantled c1680 by the Earl of Thanet. By 1773 the upper parts had fallen, and it is now very ruinous. Until recently the basement was partly buried in its own debris. The second storey is fragmentary and very little remains of the third storey. The tower was entered at ground level by a doorway closed by a portcullis in the middle of the north wall. Off the entrance passage led doors to two spiral stairs of different widths. The basement had two loops in each of the west, south and east walls. There are rooms about 2m wide and 3m to 4m long in all the corners, that on the SW having a latrine opening off it in the very corner itself. This corner has been later strengthened by a diagonally projecting turret 3m wide which contained latrines on the two upper storeys. The second storey also has evidence of loops to the west, south and east, and there were chambers in the corner, all apparently L-shaped except for that on the NE.

Pendragon has commonly been described as a late 12th century keep or tower house. Hugh de Morville is thought to have had a castle here in the 1180s, but other keeps of his era rarely have at ground level any mural rooms, latrines, or entrances nor did they usually have portcullises. In 1203 a castle here was restored to Hugh's nephew Robert de Vipont, and in c1269 it passed by marriage to Robart de Leyburne, being mentioned at the time of his death in 1283 as "the castle of Mallerstang". The existing building is most likely to be the work of Robert de Clifford, licensed to crenellate a tower here in 1309, and killed at Bannockburn in 1314. The castle was confiscated after his son Roger was executed by Edward II after being captured in the battle of Boroughbridge, but it was returned to the heir in 1323. The corner turret may be of the 1360s, when Robert de Clifford is reported to have rebuilt the tower here. The entrance with its portcullis and staircases, plus the round headed basement loops, may represent what the Countess Anne had done to the building in the 1660s.

# PENRITH CASTLE    NY 512299

John de Dreux, Duke of Brittany, granted a perpetual lease of land at Penrith to William Strickland together with the right to build a "fortalice" in which the Duke would have the right to stay if he wished. The Duke was forfeited in 1382 but de Strickland remained in possession. The "chamber" which he was licensed by Richard II to crenellate in 1397 was either the thinly walled tower 8m square with a spiral stair in the east corner, now lacking its parapet and buried within the mansion of Hutton Hall to the NW at NY 518302, or was the Strickland Tower at the castle. Only a vaulted cellar with a loop at each end remains of this tower which was 9.6m by 9m over walls 2m thick. The tower projects from the middle of the NE side of a court 36m square and protected an entrance with a drawbar-slot immediately to the south. The wall 1.5m thick around this court is probably the "mantlet of stone and lime" for which another crenellation licence was granted in 1399. The east corner contains a chamber for smoking meat and the other three corners have diagonal buttresses which supported tiny turrets. The parapet was carried on corbelling, still remaining on much of the SE and SW sides where there were mid-wall buttresses.

*Plan of Pendragon Castle*

*Plan of Penrith Castle*

*Penrith Castle*

Whatever internal buildings the castle had in its first phase must have been of wood. The existing ranges of stone were built by Ralph Neville, Earl of Westmorland, who was granted the castle by Henry IV, William Strickland having become bishop of Carlisle in 1400. The SE range contained a hall 6.3m wide and has no dividing walls, any partitions being of wood. The NE range was 7.8m wide internally and the SW range containing the kitchens was 5.6m wide internally. None of the inner walls now stand more than 2m high. There is a well in the court. A new gateway was created on the NW side and the Red Tower measuring 10m by 9.5m was built out from the north end of this side to command it. Only the NW end wall of the tower now stands above the level of the vault over the basement. After Richard Neville, Earl of Warwick, was killed at the battle of Barnet in 1471, Edward IV granted Penrith to his brother the Duke of Gloucester, later Richard III. Richard extended the new gateway, adding a block 15m by 8m containing rooms for porters or guards on either side of a central passage. The external staircase up to rooms in the NW and NE ranges were also added at this time, along with other alterations which included the heightening of the outer wall at the east end of the SE side. This provided an upper chamber above the original solar with big windows looking out towards the field.

By this time, if not before, there seems to have been an outer wall on the edge of a ditch about 20m away from the the wall of the main court. Standing in the ditch on the NE was an outer gatehouse which was "mostly collapsed" at the time of a survey of 1565. Henry VIII had materials removed the decayed castle in 1547. A second survey in 1572 describes the outer gatehouse in "utter ruin", three stables were about to collapse, and the chapel, great chamber, hall, two kitchens, and other offices were "not repairable" and "many cartloads" of stone had been removed. Despite the general decay the castle was used as a headquarters by General Lambert for a month in 1648. It was granted by William III in 1694 to his favourite the Duke of Portland. The 3rd Duke sold the castle to his brother-in-law the Duke of Devonshire and it was later sold to the Lancaster and Carlisle Railway. Penrith Urban Council acquired the ruin in 1914 and it was excavated and conserved during the 1920s.

*Penrith Castle*

## PIEL CASTLE   SD 232636   F (ferry from mainland)

This castle stands at the south end of an island guarding the entrance to the harbour of Barrow-in-Furness. The licence granted by Edward III in 1327 to John Cockerham, Abbot of Furness Abbey, for the crenellation of his "dwelling house at Fotheray" is assumed to refer to the existing keep. There is no certain evidence of an earlier castle except that when King Stephen granted all his lands in Furness and Walney to the Abbot of Furness he made it a condition that the abbot would "make, sustain, repair and guard a fort here". When Abbot John de Bolton dismantled the "pele de Fotheray" because of the cost of upkeep, Henry IV confiscated the castle on the grounds that dismantling broke the agreement with Stephen. It was returned to the Abbot in 1411 and made partly habitable in 1429. By 1537 the "Castelle and Pele" was "sore decayed, and specially the covering and timberwork therof, insomuch that £300 will scarcely repair it sufficiently". During the Civil War the Royalists considered refortifying the castle until they realised it was too ruined to easily repair. In 1660 it was granted by Charles II to George Monck, Duke of Albermarle, and in 1688 it passed to the Duke of Buccleugh. A later Duke had repairs made in 1876-8.

The castle consists of a very impressive keep surrounded by an inner ward which in turn lies in the SE corner of an outer ward just over 100m square. By 1727 the southern outer defences had been destroyed by the sea, and by 1781 the eastern wall of the inner ward and the SE corner of the keep had gone. Further erosion has now destroyed all of the inner ward south side and the entire east wall of the keep. Huge blocks of fallen masonry still remain on the beach to the south. Both wards were protected on their north and west sides by ditches and walls 2.4m thick and 4.5m high. Of the outer wall there remains the eastern half of the north side plus towers about 4.5m square at the northern corners and at a point on the SW side where the curtain turned through a shallow angle. The tower at the NE corner seems to have been a gatehouse and has remains of a chapel just south of it. At the corner between the fairly complete north and west walls of the inner ward is a small tower projecting within the court, and there are remains of larger rectangular towers at the NE and SW corners. On the west is a two storey gatehouse 6.1m square.

*Inner Curtain at Piel Castle*

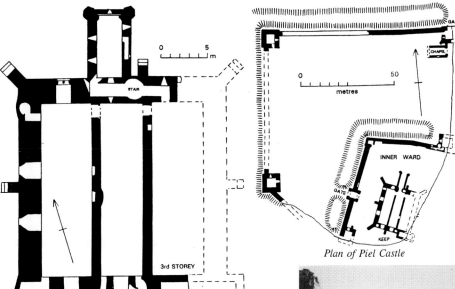

Plan of Piel Castle

Piel Castle: plan of keep

The keep measured 24.3m from north to south by 22.6m wide over walls 2.4m thick. Buttresses projecting from the sides and diagonally from three of the corners die back into octagonal turrets at the top. A projection 10m long by 4m wide at the SE corner seems to have contained latrines. Above a low basement there were two upper storeys of fine rooms with big two-light windows set in embrasures with seats. The entrance is on the north side at second storey level through an embattled two storey porch with a finely-moulded arch with a portcullis groove flanked by polygonal buttresses. At the inner end was another portcullis, a doorway to a staircase, and then one entered a central corridor

The keep, Piel Castle

4.4m wide lighted by a window only at the far south end. On either side were single chambers 5.1m wide and 18m long. Little remains of that on the east but that on the west has four windows and a fireplace near the south end of the west wall. Possibly this end was divided off by a timber partition. The third storey was similarly arranged.

## PRESTON PATRICK HALL   SD 544837

The 14th century hall block has windows with ogee-headed lights and doorways with shouldered lintels. Two lead into the east wing which has a central passage between two vaulted cellars. It is assumed that this part originally formed a three storey tower but there is now just one upper storey of c1500 with straight-headed windows with panel tracery. The west wing has a large corbelled fireplace on the upper storey. The hall passed by marriage from the Curwens to the Prestons c1530.

## RANDALHOLM HALL    NY 708485

The tower measures 8.2m by 7.7m over walls 1.5m thick. The vaulted basement has an original loop at the east end and a west doorway off which leads straight stairs. There are later sashed windows above. A spiral stair in one corner connects the second and third storeys. Access up to the fourth storey is by a straight stair in the thickness of one wall. The parapet is now replaced by a gabled overall roof. A bastle-type building is incorporated in the range NW of the tower. Randalholme was held by Robert de Vipont and was later a seat of the Whitfield family.

## ROCKCLIFFE CASTLE    NY 354619

In 1539 Leland note here "a pretty Pile or Castle of the lord Dakers". It was seized and garrisoned by Leonard Dacre during the 1569 rebellion and consequently forfeited. In c1583 the castle was ordered to be "kept as in William, Lord Dacre's time". It was acquired by Anne, Countess of Arundel c1601, and in 1603 was used as a prison for incarcerating some of the lawless Graham clan. A description of the castle in 1607 suggests it had been built by the Dacres at the beginning of the 16th century. Henry, Duke of Norfolk, sold the castle in 1682 to the Reverend Charles Usher, and it was demolished c1730 and replaced by a new house. When the adjacent road was realigned c1901 a pavement of cobbles, assumed to be the castle court, was found along with a 17m long section of sandstone walling 1.4m thick aligned north-south. This wall and the parallel wall on old foundations 28m to the east which encloses the garden of the present house are assumed to have defined the castle area.

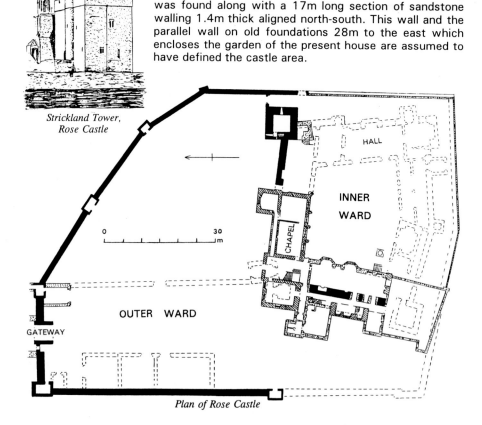

*Strickland Tower,*
*Rose Castle*

HALL

INNER

WARD

CHAPEL

OUTER   WARD

GATEWAY

0        30
m

*Plan of Rose Castle*

# ROSE CASTLE   NY 371461   V

The palace of the bishops of Carlisle stands on the site of a motte and bailey castle taken from Hervey Fitz Maurice by Henry II in 1186. The palace was occupied by Edward I and Queen Eleanor for most of September 1300. It was burnt by the Scots in 1314 and 1322, and again in 1337 whilst Bishop John Kirby (1332-53) was building a curtain wall licensed by Edward III in 1336 and also adding the Constable's Tower by the NW corner. This has gone, as have additions by Bishop Gilbert Welton (1352-62) licensed in 1355 and thought to have included the great hall and Pottinger's Tower at the SW corner. By the end of the 15th century the castle was concentric with an irregular shaped inner court with ranges on all sides and various projecting towers set in the east corner of a lozenge-shaped outer court measuring about 65m by 85m with a wall about 1.8m thick. There was an outer gate in a range with small square towers at each end. Alongside the long SW wall of the outer court were stables and a barn. A wall from the outer gate inner ward west corner closed of the NE corner as a garden. Two projections from the outer wall here contain latrines and other latrines projected from the south side of the outer court.

After capture and slighting by Parliamentary troops in 1648 it was claimed that most of the 49 rooms in the castle were wrecked. In 1650 the building was sold to William Heveningham, who occupied the few remaining usable rooms in the west range, making a new entrance through a tower 9.7m wide on this side which had been added by Bishop Kite in 1522-4. After the castle was returned to him in 1660 Bishop Stern demolished the gutted east range containing a great hall and also part of the south range containing a long gallery. In the angle between these ranges were the kitchen and further west were the brewhouse and bakehouse. Bishop Rainbow remodelled the west range in the 1660s and further work was done in the 1760s by Bishop Lyttleton, who described the castle as "a very commodious and agreeable mansion". At the north corner is the Strickland Tower, remodelled by Bishop William Strickland, (1400-19) but originally built by Bishop John de Halton (1292-1324). It contains a vaulted basement above which were two rooms, one of which was a chapel with a trefoil-headed piscina. The tower was entered at this level from the west by a doorway with a shouldered lintel. Between here and the tower added by Bishop Bell in the 1480s lay the bishop's private chamber, an apartment 12m long of which little now remains. Bishop Bell also built the chapel west of this but it was remodelled by Bishop Rainbow in the 1660s and now most of its features are of another remodelling by Thomas Rickman for Bishop Percy in 1829-31. Rickman also added a semicircular stair turret to the Strickland Tower and made considerable alterations to the west range, completely refacing the whole of the west side.

*Rose Castle*

*Scaleby Castle*

# SCALEBY CASTLE    NY 449625

Henry I granted Scaleby to Richard de Tilliol. After Cumbria was recovered from the Scots in 1157 Scaleby was restored to Richard's grandson Peter. The first record of a dwelling is in 1246 when there was "a capital messuage with houses". The tower which Robert de Tilliol was licensed to crenellate in 1307 was damaged by the Scots in 1317 but had been repaired by 1367 when Scaleby is first referred to as a castle. The hall on the east side may be of the time of Peter de Tilliol on whose death in 1435 Scaleby passed to two heiresses, Isabella Colvill and Margaret Moresby, who remodelled the domestic buildings. In the 1580s the castle was lying empty and decayed but in the 1590s it was purchased by Sir Edward Musgrave, who rebuilt the south range. A Royalist garrison held out against attacks by Parliamentary troops for several months in 1644, and they only finally surrendered after a second siege in February 1645, after or during which the castle was badly damaged. Despite this it was regarrisoned by Royalists in 1648 but quickly surrendered to General Lambert. In the 1660s the Gilpin family purchased the castle and made the south wing habitable, it being in 1685 described as "lately repaired and new modelled". It decayed after being sold to Edward Stephenson in 1741 and was ruinous by 1772. The south block was again restored after the castle was sold to Rowland Fawcett c1800. Further rebuilding was in progress in 1838. The castle was sold to James Watt in 1944 and was later acquired by Lord Henley who still occupies it.

The buildings form a compact group roughly 27m square in the middle of a platform 125m in diameter surrounded by a wet moat 12m wide. On the west are traces of an inner moat. The tower house measures 12.5m by 8.5m over walls up to 2.4m thick. The three storeys above the basement vault are ruined. All the levels were connected by a spiral stair in the SW corner. The doorway knocked through from the hall block is modern and the original entrance faced west. A polygonal forebuilding with an open court 6m in diameter was later added to help protect it.

*Scaleby Castle*

West of the forebuilding is a curtain wall 10.6m long and 2.4m thick containing an entrance with an almost round outer archway. The inner arch has a sunk quadrant moulding of early 14th century date. The passage was closed by a portcullis and door and flanked by guard chambers, that to the west being L-shaped and occupying the base of a turret facing NW. On the east side of the court is a vaulted cellar (now subdivided, below a hall 11.2m long by 6.4m wide, later heightened with new upper windows. The south range is 27m long by 7.6m wide and contains four rooms on each of three storeys. The outer wall with projecting turrets at each end and in the middle has 14th century work at the base but the range is otherwise of c1597-1600 with a projection towards the court containg a spiral staircase beside the entrance. The windows mostly date from Thomas Rickman's remodelling in the late 1830s.

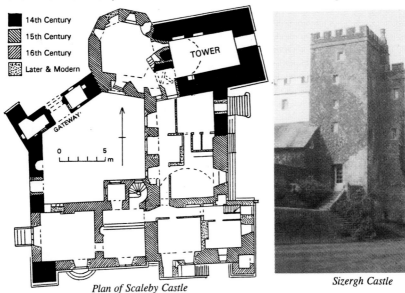

■ 14th Century
▨ 15th Century
▨ 16th Century
▧ Later & Modern

TOWER

GATEWAY

0    5
⌊⌊⌊⌊⌊⌊⌋ m

*Plan of Scaleby Castle*

*Sizergh Castle*

## SHANK CASTLE   NY 469704

Above the River Lyne stood a four storey tower which was ruined by 1777 and demolished in 1951. Probably built c1600, it is first mentioned in 1618 as the dwelling of the Earl of Cumberland's steward William Hutton. The tower measured 15.8m by 9m over walls up to 1.5m thick, and was 12m high. The main entrance lay in the SE wall at the level of the second storey 3m above ground. Another doorway on the SW led into the basement which had a spiral stair to the second storey. Each level was divided into three equal parts by crosswalls. From the middle room on the second storey a spiral stair rose in the NW wall to the upper storeys lighted by two-light windows.

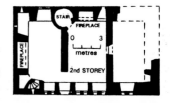

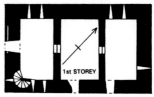

*Shank: plans*

## SIZERGH CASTLE   SD 499879   O

Sizergh has belonged to the Strickland family since 1239 but is now in the custody of the National Trust. The oldest part is a four storey tower of about 1340 with a main body 18.7m long from NW to SE by 10.8m wide over walls up to 2.2m thick in the lower part. A wing 6.5m wide projecting 3.7m from the SW wall contains chambers, that at third storey level having a latrine. A smaller turret on the NE side contains a spiral stair connecting with upper and lower entrances on either side of the turret. Both the turret and wing rise high above the main parapets. There must have always been a subdivision of each level of the tower but the present walls dividing the two vaulted cellars and the Queen's Room from the Dining Room on the second storey are 16th century and the lath and plaster divisions above are still later. The fireplace of the hall on the third storey is original. This room now rises through the fourth storey as well with a gallery connecting the room at the south end with the staircase. Several other fireplaces are 16th century and there are 15th century windows in each end wall at third storey level. On the second storey is a Venetian window at the SE end and a five-light window at the NW end which are part of alterations carried out c1770 for Cecilia Towneley, wife of Charles Strickland.

*Sizergh Castle*

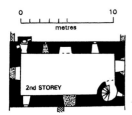

*Plan of Skelsmergh Hall*

A hall-block east of the tower was replaced by a new hall in the 16th century. Of about the same time are the cross-wing to the NE containing a vaulted lower room and two other long ranges which form the NE and SW sides of a court. All these parts have seen much alteration and the hall now has a room over with symmetrical layout of the 1770s with recesses on either side of a doorway from a staircase lobby on the NW and three regularly spaced sash windows facing out towards the terrace overlooking the lawns and pools on the SE. Plaster chimneypieces in the Elizabethan parts are dated 1563, 1564, 1569, and 1575.

## SKELSMERGH HALL    SD 531959

The NW wing is the three storey tower of the Leyburne family now lacking its parapets. The tower measures 12.4m by 6.6m with side walls 1.5m thick thinning to 1.2m above the vault over the cellar. There is an entrance on the south side which seems to have had a straight stair leading towards the base of the spiral stair in the SE corner. Only two beams remain of the third storey floor. This storey retains original end windows with pairs of ogival-headed lights under a square head with a moulded label. The second storey has a latrine in a projection near the NW corner, a fireplace and narrow loops on the north and wider windows to east and south. The position of a loop at the west end of the south wall suggests that there was once a hall block to the south. The existing parlour wing projecting from the east end of the south wall is late 16th century. Projecting east from this, and on a different alignment, is a larger early 17th century wing with a kitchen at the far end and a scale-and-platt staircase on the north side. Reset on the modern porch in the SW re-entrant angle is part of the head of a fireplace with the date 1629.

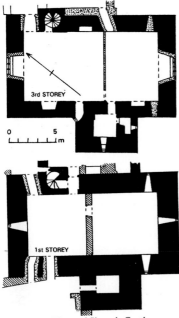

*Plans of Sizergh Castle*

*Shank Castle*

## SMARDALE HALL    NY 739082

A rectangular platform by the hall may be the site of the house of the de Smardales. They are thought to have built the tower shown on a plan of c1670. It passed by marriage c1580 from the Warcop family to the Dalstons who built a long block with round corner turrets some way west of the tower. This survives and has no defensive features. It is more Scottish than English. The SE turret contains a spiral staircase. Another range later joined the two parts, between which was a court. Further works were executed for Sir George Dalston after he settled here in 1761.

## STONEHAUGH TOWER    NY 463804

The lower parts of the NW and SW walls remain of a tower 10m by 7m over walls 1.5m thick with two original loops. The tower is shown on a map of 1590 and a "platt" of 1607. It was the seat of Robert Forster who died in 1598.

## TEBAY MOTTES    NY 600054 & 613051    V

At the confluence of the the Dorothy and Birk becks is what appears to be an unfinished motte with a summit 23m by 9m, isolated to the east by a ditch. West of Tebay is a motte rising 6m to a summit 34m across, its northern slope having been eroded by a stream. A ditch 6m wide and 2m deep divides it from a U-shaped bailey to the south measuring 133m by 61m and 2m high above the surrounding land. This was probably the seat of the Tebay family in the 12th century.

## THISTLEWOOD TOWER    NY 396436    V

The house lies on the west bank of the Rose Beck and comprises a tower house with mullioned windows and an adjoining 17th century block of five bays with two-light windows. The tower measures 7.5m by 5.8m over walls 1.1m thick and has original entrances to both of the two lowest storeys, the upper doorway having a shouldered lintel suggesting a 14th century date. The basement has a barrel-vault.

## THORNTHWAITE HALL    NY 513163

Lord William Howard may have added a wing to this tower built by the Curwen family after he acquired it in the early 17th century. The building is L-shaped with mullioned windows, the tower having a six-light window at ground level. Now gabled instead of embattled and used to contain a staircase, it measures 9.2m by 8m over walls up to 1.4m thick. In the early 18th century it passed by marriage to John Warwick and was sold to Edward Hasell of Dalemain.

*Tebay Motte*

## TRIERMAIN CASTLE   NY 595669

Edward III granted Roland de Vaux a licence to crenellate this building in 1340. The remains lie on a mound with traces of a ditch 6m wide. The one remaining 9m high fragment (patched up by the Earl of Carlisle in the 1920s) was the SE corner of the northern of two wings 5.4m wide projecting at either end of a block 19.6m long by 7.6m wide over walls 1.6m thick. This wing formerly had a stone with the Vaux arms. There was a tower on the the east side of a court to the east until it was dismantled c1688. During Edward IV's reign the castle passed by marriage to Sir Richard Salkeld. Thomas, Lord Dacre, won a dispute with Richard's heiresses over ownership c1510. It decayed, especially after the Dacres' forfeiture in 1569, and reports of the 1580s describe it in a ruinous condition. A considerable part of the ruin collapsed in 1832 and the materials were used to repair adjacent farm buildings.

## UBARROW HALL   NY 504026

The 15th century tower measures 9m by 6.2m over walls 1.5m thick at the level of the vaulted basement. The storeys above are connected by a spiral stair in the SE corner and are reached by an outside stair on the south. In the 17th century the old hall-block to the east was replaced by a wing almost as wide as the tower is long. Ubarrow was a Leyburne seat but passed by marriage to the Harringtons.

*Ubarrow: plan*

## ULPHA OLD HALL   SD 182924   V

This tower may have been built as late as c1580-1620 as the fragmentary remains of its basement indicate a layout more typical of the Jacobean period than the medieval period. The building measures 14.8m by 8.8m over walls 1.2m thick except that the east wall is thickened to 1.6m to accommodate two fireplaces at ground level and another two higher up. The entrance between the lower fireplaces has been modernised. From it led a passage across the building to a staircase in a wing 5.4m wide at the back. The wing has narrow loops flanking the adjacent walls.

*Plan of Ulpha Old Hall*

*Ulpha Old Hall*

*Triermain Castle*

## WARCOP CASTLE  NY 750154

The name Castle Hill marks the spot of the seat of the de Warcop family. A 17th century antiquary reported having seen walls dug up and masonry from the site is said to have been taken to build the tower of Kirkby Stephen church c1506. The vicarage to the NW once had a surrounding moat of which traces remain, whilst Warcop Tower Farm perpetuates the name of a former tower of the Warcop and then the Fairer families to the SW. Warcop Hall is an unfortified 16th century house.

## WEST NEWTON  NY 130437

The de Newtons are thought to have had their seat here from c1130 until Edward III's reign. Earthworks define a court 40m by 28m with mounds possibly covering the collapsed remains of towers at the western corners. Scarps and ditches mark out an outer court measuring 70m by 60m to the west.

## WHARTON HALL  NY 770062  V

The Wharton family built a modest hall block with cross-wings at each end in the early 15th century. The SW face is all-embattled and the NW wing is of three storeys and can be regarded as a solar-tower. It contains a staircase of c1700. The porch and the lower rooms of the SE cross-wing are vaulted. These rooms flank a passage which now leads to the site of a larger new hall 18.5m long by 8m wide built c1540 by Thomas, 1st Lord Wharton. The SW wall of this hall is reduced to foundations but the opposite wall retains a fireplace in a projecting breast and parts of a projecting bay. At the SE end of this hall lies a cross-wing also of the 1540s containing a cellar and an upper kitchen with fireplaces on the NE and SE sides and transomed three-light windows facing SW. To the SW of the two halls and their cross-wings lies a court enclosed by an impressive gatehouse range of 1559 on the SW with a spiral stair in a turret rising originally to two upper storeys, another 16th century range on the NE, and a wall on the south side now without buildings abutting it.

*Gatehouse, Wharton Hall*

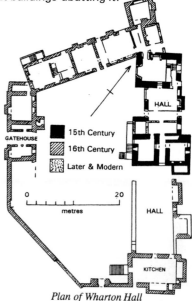

*Plan of Wharton Hall*

## WHITEHALL   NY 202416

An embattled three storey tower or stronghouse 13m by 7.6m over walls 1.4m thick was later extended 7.8m to the north. The later part has on the east side a stone dated 1589 with arms and an inscription relating to Laurence Salkeld. The house was described as ruinous in 1794 but is currently inhabited. Fragments remain of considerable extensions to the west by Salvin for George Moore in 1861-2. Not far to the east is an older small moated platform.

*Whitehall*

## WOLSTEY CASTLE   NY 104506

By a bend of a stream is a moated platform about 30m square on which lie grass-covered foundations and blocks of fallen masonry. This was probably the manor house of "Wolmsty" which the Abbot of Holme Cultram Abbey was licensed by Edward III to crenellate in 1348. It was intended as a secure place where treasure, books, and charters could be kept safe from Scottish raids. The Chambers family long had custody of it although it was ruinous by 1572 when a survey refers to "all the houses within the outer wall" comprising a "hall with a chamber attached, the Evidence house, the kitchen, the peat house, byer and the stable". A report of 1580 mentions that "this house or castle belongs to Her Majesty, its keeper, Thomas Chambers should repair it". The local inhabitants offered to pay for repairs in 1581 but in 1583 it was placed in the care of Robert Chambers "with the fee of 20 shillings yearly, for the keeping therof", although in practice he had to spend some of his own money as well on repairing the castle. In the 1640s it passed by marriage to Thomas Barwis and was damaged during the Civil Wars, being ruinous in 1649. Thomas Fitch, Governor of Carlisle, had the castle demolished in 1652, some materials being taken to repair the defences at Carlisle and other parts used to build a house at Hayrigg 2km to the east. In 1654 the list of buildings demolished mentions "The Hall, one tower at the end of the Hall, one great barn, one Larder House, one long gallery, one chapel with a chamber at the end, one chamber called Michael Scots' chamber (he was a noted wizard who flourished c1175-1235), one house called the prison, one tower above the said house, one long byer, and one great stable", and it also refers to "the ruins of the walls of the castle". By 1913 only one fragment of walling about 2m thick remained on the northern side of the court.

*NW range, Wharton Hall*

*Workington Hall*

## WORKINGTON HALL    NY 008288    O

Patrick de Curwen is said to have transferred here during King John's reign from a possible earlier fortified site at "Burrow Walls" 1km to the NNW. The building stands on a platform above the south side of the Derwent at the east end of the town. The three storey tower house in the SE corner must be the "house at Wyrkyngton" which Richard II licensed Gilbert de Curwen IV to crenellate in 1380, and which is called a castle in 1402. The tower measures 13.1m by 10.3m over walls up to 2.7m thick. It has a vaulted basement but the large arched windows in both the tower and the hall block north of it are of 1782-1828, when the upper parts, now demolished, were rebuilt. The gatehouse in the west range may also be late 14th century. The hall in the east range is of c1540, but perhaps incorporating earlier parts, and also of that period is the kitchen range north of it, with a turret projecting diagonally from its NE corner. In 1568 Sir Henry Curwen gave refuge at the hall to Mary, Queen of Scots when she landed here after fleeing from Scotland. The south and north ranges linking the gatehouse to the eastern parts are of c1597-1600 but there has been much Georgian remodelling with angle pavilions added on the western corners. The house passed from the Curwens to the Chance family c1930 and was presented to the town in 1946 but allowed to decay. The shell has recently been consolidated.

*Tower at Yanwath Hall*

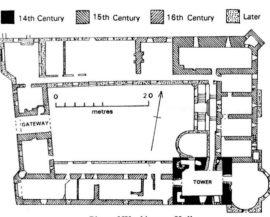

■ 14th Century  ▨ 15th Century  ▨ 16th Century  ▨ Later

*Plan of Workington Hall*

*Wraysholme; plan*

*Yanworth: plans*

*Wraysholme Tower*

## WRAYSHOLME TOWER    SD 383754

The Harringtons built this tower in the late 15th century. It measures 12.4m by 8.7m over walls 1.4m thick. A thicker part of the west wall contains the entrance with a spiral stair adjoining in the SW corner. Latrines are contained in a projection from the east end of the south wall. Originally of three storeys with battlements and turrets, the building now contains just a store over a cowhouse. A farmhouse of 1848 stands on the site of a hall-block on the west side.

## WYTHOP HALL    NY 202284

The hall of 1678 may stand on or near the site of a house of Hugh de Lowther which Edward II licensed him to crenellate in 1318. It may have been rebuilt in the mid 16th century and whatever stood on the site before 1678 was "ruinated" in 1671.

## YANWATH HALL    NY 508282

The house has a a south range of the 14th and 15th centuries, a 15th century east range and a 17th century north range containing the courtyard entrance and stables. The hall lies in the middle of the south range with the kitchen east of it and the tower forming a solar block west of it. The kitchen retains a 15th century fireplace in the east wall but the north and south walls were rebuilt in the 17th century. The hall has a 15th century bay window at the west end which is now divided off to form a separate room. The hall fireplace backing onto the screens passage between it and the kitchen is a 16th century insertion. The tower measures 11.2m by 9.3m over walls from 1.6m to 2m thick. The vaulted basement is 14th century but the upper two storeys and the battlements with an ornamental moulding and small square corner turrets are later, possibly as late as the Elizabethan period to which the five-light mullioned windows on three sides of the second storey certainly belong. This storey has a latrine in the NW corner, a fireplace in the east wall with the arms of Elizabeth I above it, and a plaster ceiling with an openwork pendant at the intersection of the beams. The room above has more modestly sized windows on all four sides, a fireplace on the west, and small rooms in the SE and NW corners, the latter having a slop drain. There are also lockers in the east and west walls. Yanwath was held by the Suttons and Threlkelds and passed by marriage to Lord Dudley c1520. It was sold to the Lowther family in 1654.

# OTHER CASTLES AND TOWERS IN CUMBRIA

ABBEY FLATTS NY 052075 A natural mound has possibly converted into a motte 30m across on top with a bailey 28m wide on the west side.

ABBEYTOWN NY 177509 The earthwork north of the abbey may be a motte raised by Alan FitzWaldeve or part of a late 12th century precinct rampart.

ARTHURET KNOWES NY 381674 Tower mentioned in 1542, shown on 1552 map. Possibly the tower at Longtown shown on 1590 map was the same building.

BANK HEAD NY 368708 Vanished tower, not on 1590 map but shown on 1607 platt. Captured by Buccleugh in 1596 despite having a yett and plenty of stores. David Graham of Bankhead was deported as a malefactor in 1606.

BLEATARN NY 467611 House on footings of Hetheringtons' stronghouse of c1600.

BOLTONGATE NY 229406 Tower 6.7m by 5.8m on east side of rectory. Segmental-vaulted basement with one north loop and just one upper storey.

BOWNESS-ON-SOLWAY NY 224625 Old Rectory blown up c1860 had tower 9.4m by 6.2m. Vaulted basement with loop each end and doorway with drawbar slot to north. Later wing on south side projected to east.

BRAES NY 573752 Ruinous in 1854 and now gone. Said to have been a tower 9m square over walls 1.5m thick with court on the south side.

BRAMPTON NY 510616 Thinly walled 14th century cross-wing at Old Church Farm. A stronghouse once stood immediately east of the Moot Hall in village.

BRAYSTONES NY 009058 Seat of de Braystones family until 14th century. Bailey platform 85m by 38m above Ehen. 19th century tower on site of motte.

BROUGHAM HALL NY 527283 Large ruin of various dates. 16th century gatehouse. Sales to John Bird 1676, to Broughams 1724, to Carleton-Coopers in 1934.

BURROW WALLS NY 003300 Defaced east wall 13 long and north wall 4.6m long and 1.3m thick with traces of spiral stair in corner. On site of Roman Fort.

CAMERTON HALL NY 033306 House built 1833 by Cook family on site of and perhaps incorporates remains of older house or tower of Curwen family.

CARDEW HALL NY 337491 Denton family seat looks 16th century. Possibly older.

CASTLE CARROCK NY 544554 Platform 90m by 45m with ditch 6m wide east of church may be site of seat of Gamel de Castlecarrock in the 1160s.

*Castlehaugh, Sedbergh*

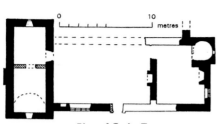

*Plan of Crake Trees*

*Ubarrow Hall*

CASTLEHAUGH SD 662923 Robert de Mowbray may have built this motte on a hill above Sedbergh c1090. It rises 8m above a ditch 5m wide to a summit about 12m by 15m. A bailey platform 30m by 23m lies to the west.

CONEYSIDE COP NY 982094 Mound, perhaps mostly natural, with bank and ditch.

COUPLAND NY 709189 Possible ringwork 18m across, 2m high outside, 1m inside.

CRAKE TREES NY 617155 Ruin. Thinly walled south wing 9.8m by 4.8m with vaulted cellar possibly a reduced 14th century tower. Hall and north solar block with spiral stair in one corner are mostly 15th and 16th century.

CROSBY-ON-EDEN NY 448596 Church and churchyard on site of possible motte with crescent-shaped bailey.

CUNSWICK SD 485933 Early 16th century gatehouse remains but tower taken down during a remodelling of the hall block c1582. Leyburn seat until 1715.

CRUMMOCK WATER NY 149202 Footings of building of uncertain date by lake.

CUMCROOK NY 504749 Routledge seat beside River Lyne raided 1583 and 1592. It and tower at NY 490740 both on 1590 map. Present house of 1685.

DALTON SD 539753 Fragment of old tower said to adjoin 17th century house.

DERWENTWATER Family of that name had seat by Castle Lane in 1220s. Passed to Radcliffes 1317. Thinly walled house on Lord's Isle in lake built c1460. Wings added in 17th century, destroyed 1709, overgrown footings remain.

DOCKWRAY HALL SD 513934 Tower perhaps destroyed in 1650s when Dockwray family forfeited. Part may have survived in barn until early 20th century.

DUNMALLOGHT PELE NY 467247 The site fortified and garrisoned by William de Dacre under the terms of his licence of 1307 may have been Dacre or at or near this hillfort on a wooded hill at the NE end of Ullswater.

EDENHALL NY 564323 Mansion of 1797 and 1820s replaced tower and hall-block. William de Stapleton had a "fortlet on the water of Eamont in 1349.

GLASSON BARRACKS NY 253605 Altered and inhabited stronghouse 13.2m by 6.6m over walls 1m thick. Spiral stair with blocked loop in south corner. Doorway and loop on NW, two other original loops on SE. Restored 1982.

GRANGE HALL NY 684109 Grange of Byland Abbey, 14th century, with 15th century oriel and 17th century round stair turret corbelled out over west corner. Panel on NW side with Bellingham arms. Later extensions, etc.

GREAT SALKELD NY 552366 Rectory is much altered hall block with small tower. Datestone of 1674 with initials of Thomas Musgrave, later Dean of Carlisle.

HAILE HALL NY 038093 Thinly walled tower 9m by 7m and 16th century range to north in 18th century mansion. 1591 datestone with Ponsonby arms.

HAMPSFIELD SD 395804 Tower measuring 11m by 7m built by Thornburghs was destroyed by tenant c1814. It lay east of the hall rebuilt c1636.

HELLBECK NY 792158 18th century building on site of tower. Manor passed from Helbecks to Blenkinsops in 1320, sold to Arthur Scaife c1657.

Ringwork at Maryport

Netherhall

HEVERSHAM SD 494832 14th century hall of Wyndesores family rebuilt by Buskells
in 1540s. Thin wall beyond to north may be relic of tower then abandoned.

HUTTON HALL NY 518302 Tower 8m square over walls 1m thick adjoins house at
Penrith. Spiral stair projects with the east corner. Possibly the tower William
Strickland was licensed to embattle in 1397 & 1399. No battlements remain.

KERSHOPE NY 477821 Slight traces of moat. Tower shown on 1590 map. The
1604 survey records John Foster living at "Kirsop foote".

KILLINGTON SD 612891 Pickerings' 15th century hall block with possible narrow
tower wing of same date in ruins on west side. East cross-wing gone.

KIRKBY LONSDALE NY 611789 Motte 6m high, dished summit 24m across, on the
west bank of the Lune north of the vicarage. East side damaged.

KIRKCAMBECK NY 533689 Churchyard occupies possible triangular ringwork 2m
high with sides 43m long. Edward I stayed here three nights in March 1307.
No remains of a motte recorded at Howdale Farm 1km to the west in 1923.

KIRKOSWALD COLLEGE NY 554411 Thinly walled late 15th century tower 8m
square with wide spiral stair projecting internally. Bears arms of Sir Thomas
Dacre. Encased in later building. No vault. Originally of four storeys.

LORTON HALL NY 152257 Present thinly walled embattled tower probably 19th
century, but perhaps stands on site of a medieval tower house. Adjoining
range with seven bays of mullioned windows with pediments dated 1663.

LOW HOUSE NY 534739 Buried footings of building 14m by 12m, walls about 1.4m
thick, with later extensions, to east of derelict farmhouse.

LOW TODHOLES NY 519770 Supposed site of tower mentioned in 1510 and 1553.
Thomas Routledge of "Todholles" captured during raid by Elliots in 1581.
Alan Routledge was killed by the Armstrongs in 1583. Richard Routledge
became a fugitive after killing Nichol Hutcheson in 1618.

MARYPORT NY 033362 Ringwork 26m by 18m and 6m high above ditch on end
of spur in neck of loop of River Ellen on side south of town. Bailey to north?

MAULD'S MEABURN NY 624171 17th and 18th century buildings on site of hall and
tower. Datestones of 1610 and 1693, latter with Lowther arms.

MILLEES NY 389723 William Graham is said to have built the tower shown on the
1607 platt. It is not shown on the 1590 map although supposedly earlier.

MILLRIGG NY 608284 Walls 1m thick probably of stronghouse. Doorway of 1597.
Belonged to Birkbecks, then passed to Dalstons. The "new castle of Culchet"
from which David I of Scotland issued a charter c1141 was in this vicinity.

MOSSTHORN NY 515734 Site of tower or bastle. A lintel dated 1604 with arms and initials of a Musgrave discovered. Held by Atkinson family 1665.

MOTE NY 399738 Marked on 1552 map as a "tower and houses of ffergus Grame", also on 1590 and 1607 surveys. Latter shows second tower at NY 409735.

NETHERHALL SD 436892 Harringtons' altered 15th century block with thick walls including straight staircase. 17th century kitchen wing to north.

NETHER LEVENS SD 488851 Sold to Wilson of Dallam 1694. Then had three 16th century ranges of two storeys and curtain wall on fourth side. Ruined south range on site of medieval tower. Panel dated 1594 with Preston initials.

NOOK NY 520777 Slight traces of tower or bastle at Charter Trees, said to have had gunloops like those at Crew Castle. Routledge seat burnt in raid in 1587.

PENNINGTON SD 258777 Ringwork 48m by 44m traversed by public path on spur by Castle Farm. Seat of Pennington family until transfer c1242 to Muncaster.

RAVENSTONE NY 719045 Motte probably site of pre-1150 manor-house.

ST BEES NX 969121 In 1703 a wall was built "where ye Old Tower was pull'd Down". The tower was perhaps the prior's residence and is shown by Grose as having a roof within a parapet and standing SW of the priory church.

SCALES HALL NY 426400 Once had a moat. Datestones of 1491 and 1591 on main block. Mullioned windows with arched lights. Others with transoms. Small gatehouse of the 1580s. Outer court added in 1724.

SOCKBRIDGE NY 503259 West wing of c1550 and south wing of c1575 still remain but late 14th century tower on east side demolished in 1830 for materials to rebuild a lodge in Lowther Park. Lancasters, to Lowthers 1638.

STONEGARTHSIDE HALL NY 480819 House with hall and small court flanked by wings 7m wide and 14m long. The outer walls all 1.2m thick, probably 16th century but features later. John Forster spent £1,600 on alterations and erected the datestone of 1684. One original lower loop on the north side.

TARN HOUSE NY 605584 The east end of the house perhaps formed a tower about 8m square over walls 1.5m thick. Other thick walls further west. Refered to a new house in the inquest post mortem of Humphrey Dacre, 1485.

WARNELL HALL NY 350413 House had defensible court to SE. No trace or reliable account of tower supposedly built by Thomas Denton from ramsom of Scottish noble taken at Flodden in 1513, but a gatehouse survives.

WESTHALL NY 568677 Earthwork recognised as a motte in late 1970s.

WHELP NY 637256 Built by landowner called Whelp from Roman stones within Roman fort in early 12th century. Stone taken in 15th century to build Kirkby Thore Hall, and in 1676-9 to build the first stone bridge at Troutbeck.

WINTERSHIELDS NY 557724 Site of tower of Anthons Edward Armstrong, demolished in the 1590s by Lord Scrope as a "Hold and Receptacle for Robbers and Out-lawed Persons with which the Country was then infested".

WOODSIDE NY 433499 Tower supposedly discovered when mansion planned in 1870s for Mr Arlosh. Plan now lost and house demolished.

Towers now vanished are reported to have stood at Coatflatt NY 622059, Colby NY 665206, Gale NY 629364, Haresceugh NY 510428, Lamrick SD 599947 Rosgill Shap NY 536164, Selewra NY 410399, Whitrigg NY 226579.

A map of 1590 shows other long-lost towers such as Burnfoot NY 368661, Bush NY 335730, Cardurnock NY 172589, Cliffe NY 415661, Combe NY 337721, Greenrigg NY 332729, Guards NY 332667, Harperhill NY 500715, Luckens NY 493726, Millhill NY 332673, Mossband NY 350654, Ridings NY 408750, Rosetrees NY 356668, Rutherford NY 452788, Skinburness NY 128559, Soutermoor NY 488711, Thomwathill NY 350649, Troughhead NY 481751, Waingatehead NY 455692 Whiteclose NY 468709.

*Moat at Aldingham*

# MOATED SITES  Several other sites are mentioned elsewhere in the text.

BOLTONS  NY 209415  Well preserved, except where road adjoins at NW corner.
CREWGARTH  NY 601348  Pentagonal double ditched enclosure.
EASTFIELD SYKE  NY 766161  Moated platform first identified in 1990.
EMBLETON  NY 155292  Ditches remain on north and south sides of platform.
HALL GARTH  SD 660914  Slight traces of moat. Foundations discovered in 1890.
     Well containing late medieval pottery discovered in 1957.
HALL HILL  NY 714467  Top of morraine mound used as moated platform. Partly
     eroded by River Tyne. Fragments of decayed brick visible on site.
HALLSTEADS  NY 393343  Moated platform with causeway across NE corner of
     ditch. Possibly a building on west side.
INFELL  NY 060061  Moated site, perhaps site of a grange of Calder Abbey.
NEWTON REIGNY  NY 481315  Earthworks, site of manor house of de Reigny family.
OVERWATER  NY 247344  Almost square enclosure with entrance on one side.
SETTERAH PARK  NY 514212  House on site of that mentioned in 1459 indenture
     with traces of enclosing moat. Park mentioned in 1290.
SNITTLEGARTH  NY 216374  Moat referred to by deed of Robert de Tilliol, 1367.
SWATES  NY 555668  Possible moated platform by river.
TROSTERMONT  NY 454233  Large ditched enclosure on south shore of Ullswater.
Vanished moats: Aikton Hall NY 281528, Collinson's Castle NY 459379, Monk's Hall
     NY 202330, Netherhall Park NY 043366, Weary Hall NY 216418

*Moat at Whitehall*

# BASTLE HOUSES

Borderers in the 16th century owed allegiance to their clan rather than the English or Scottish monarchs or their nobles and officials. Their wealth lay in cattle which during the long dark winter nights were likely to be stolen by members of any other clan from either side of the border. The burning of farms and violence were common and it was easier to get revenge by a return raid than to obtain justice. The buildings listed in this section are of a specific type which came into fashion c1590 as an answer to this problem. The border ceased to have political importance after 1603 and by 1610 there was peace, the chief trouble-makers having been imprisoned, executed, or moved elsewhere, but once established the type seems to have remained in vogue until the 1650s, after which non-defensible buildings with larger windows were normal. The word bastle is derived from the French word bastille meaning a stronghold. The term was used by the early 16th century to describe defensible buildings which were not embattled and usually only of two storeys.

Bastles often occur in groups or are intervisible at a distance for mutual support. They were a tower and barmkin in one for tenant farmers. They are of mortared stone and contain a byre for livestock at ground level, with a single living room above. Bastles are thus quite different from towers of three or more storeys built by those of higher rank. Previously tenant farmers had single storey houses built either of tree trunks with a turf covering or dry stone with crude openings without cut stones. A few bastles in Northumberland have vaulted byres but each of the Cumbrian bastles had huge beams carrying a timber floor in which was a hatch so that the person who secured the drawbar of the doorway at one end of the byre (which had no windows) could get up into the living room. Normally the living room would have its own separate doorway in a sidewall just around the corner from the byre doorway. There would be a timber outside ladder which could be hauled up during a raid, the stone steps now often present being a later addition. On either side of the upper entrance would be windows no bigger than 0.4m square usually secured with iron stanchions, and at the far end would be a fire under a timber and plaster hood, the hearth being set on a stone ledge corbelled out from the far end wall. Mural fireplaces and staircases are rare in bastles, and none of them have latrines. All current roofs on bastles are slates or stone but turves or heather thatch may have been common originally. The selection of the bastles listed below are only equipped for a passive defence. They had no battlements, machicolations or flanking turrets, and gunloops only occur at High Grains, and also Crew Castle (see page 44).

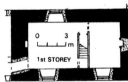
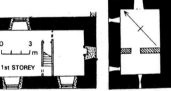

*Denton Foot: plan*  *High Grains*

*Vicar's Pele at Upper Denton*

*Bastle at Blackpool Gate*

# SELECTIVE GAZETTEER OF BASTLE HOUSES IN CUMBRIA

ANGUSWELL (Hethersgill), Carlisle  NY 472660 Armoral datestone of 1599 on later
    dovecote perhaps came from former thick-walled barn opposite farmhouse.

BLACKPOOL GATE, Bewcastle  NY 536778  One end wall 1.5m high with low
    narrow doorway with later ruined building adjoining.

BLAGILL, Alston NY 739474 Building 5.9m by 5.2m may have been a small tower
    later extended at each end by other buildings of bastle type.

BRACKENRIGG NY 232614  Home of John Glaisters 1589. Initials W.G. on roll-
    moulded doorway into barn 9.9m by 6.5m with walls 1m thick with several
    original loops. Upper storey has fireplace at SW end.

BRACKENTWAITE NY 546531  Two walls in later barn of bastle with reset lintel
    dated 1612 with initials H.A. Holes for grilles on upper windows.

CLARGHYLL HALL NY 725493 Two bastles in line both 6.2m wide with east lower
    entrances with drawbar slots. Now connected by 17th-18th century rooms.
    West bastle retains original beams supporting stone flagged upper floor.
    Third storey and steep roof giving tower-like appearence 1860s. Oriel and
    porch with forestair on east. Other bastle ruinous since fire 1889 in chapel
    built above it in 1860s. Home of Whitfields 1575 until 1802. Photo page 3.

CORBY GATES NY 733471 Building 6.5m square, walls 1m thick, in line of barns.

COTE HOUSE NY 475524 Two bastle type buildings 6.8m wide. SE one is 14.3m
    long with walls 1.2m thick, now incorporated in a farmhouse.

CUMCATCH, Brampton NY 547611 Remains of "faire stonehouse" mentioned in
    Gilsland Survey in 1603 incorporated into farm buildings. 6.6m long
    fragment of east wall with one window.

DENTON FOOT, Nether Denton NY 572623 Still inhabited, 12.6m by 7.2m. Blocked
    lower doorway at each end. Upper doorway on south also blocked and lintel
    reused on window. It has date 1594 and initials of Christopher Bell, recorded
    as tenant of 26 acres here in 1603. Two small windows remain on north.
    Tiny east window at top suggests there was an attic in roof.

HAITHWAITE, Penton NY 444772 Bastle 14.5m by 7m wide with walls up to 1.3m
    thick. Shown as tower 1590 map and house on 1607 platt. Now farmhouse.

HALL COTTAGES, Farlam  NY 570600 Two cottages near hall made out of much
    altered building 21m long, possibly original hall.

HIGH GRAINS, Askerton  NY 586753  9.1m by 6.8m, Walls 1.5m thick and 1.8m
    high. NE entrance with chamfered jambs and draw-bar slot. Three stones for
    hearth support. Crosswall perhaps later insertion. Three gunloops.

HIGH LOVELADY SHIELD, Alston  NY 759461  Collapsing square building with
    inserted mullioned window dated 1691 on lintel. Extension dated 1720. Both
    stones also have initials of members of the Watson family.

HOLMEHEAD, Burtholme NY 569638 Altered bastle 11.8m by 7.3m, walls 1m thick.

HILL HOUSE, Farlam  NY 644593 Two walls with loops remain in ruined farmhouse.

KILNSTOWN, Bewcastle  NY 535741  Slight remains of footings in present house.

LONNING HEAD, Alston, NY 747417 Much altered, now three storey holiday home.

LOW GRAINS, Bewcastle NY 576750 Doorway with rounded jambs is main relic of
    bastle 9.2m by 6.9m over walls 1.4m thick.

NEW GARTH, Farlam  NY 580606 John Hall was tenant here in 1603. Bastle much
    altered in late 17th and 19th centuries. Side walls partly original.

PEEL O'HILL, Bewcastle NY 558753 10m by 7m, walls 1.2m thick, incorporated in
    house. Boiler recess in 1.5m thick east wall probably marks former doorway.
    In 1618 a Survey of Disordered Persons cites Patrick Storey of Peel O'Hill
    as "surpassing all the theeves in Bewcastle" " for stealing" and "receiting".

STONEHOUSE, Naworth Park NY 572626 Ruined superior bastle 16.4m by 7.1m, walls 4.6m high. SW end wall rebuilt. Lower doorway and one loop on NW side, two loops and one barred window on SE side, another barred window on NE. Upper storey has fireplace in projecting breast and three windows on NW, window and fireplace at NE end and mullioned window on SE.

TALKIN HEAD, Gilsland NY 555559 Lower part of bastle 8.9m by 6.5m. Loop in 1.3m thick south end wall. Lintel from north doorway lies on ground.

TEMON, Upper Denton NY 617638 15m by 7.3m, in outbuildings by house of c1700. Belonged to Lamb family. Upper storey has two windows with grilles of two stanchions and four horizontal bars in each of north and south walls. Other window beside fireplace in west wall. Blocked window beside doorway on south side. There is a shute in a recess in the north wall.

THE LOAN, Bewcastle NY 561785 One end wall with doorway with chamfered jambs and drawbar slot incorporated at one end of a later cottage.

TOWNHEAD, Ainstable NY 562490 12.6m by 7.7m still in use. Slightly heightened and roof pitch reduced. Four windows (three blocked) and side doorway on upper storey original. Fireplace in projecting breast at SW end also original. Altered lower doorway also in sidewall, an unusual position. This tenement held by the Grahams was unusually large, hence the superior features.

VICAR'S PELE, Upper Denton NY 615654. 8.4m by 7m over walls 1.2m thick. Lower storey has loop at each end and doorway with chamfered jambs and drawbar slot on north side. Upper storey rather altered but seems to have also had doorway on north. Fireplace in west wall.

WHITE HOUSE FARM, Glassonby NY 577389 Bastle 11m by 7m by outbuildings. South wall has original lower doorway with corbels either side internally to carry beam to support longitudinal beam. Upper storey has three original windows to east, two windows and doorway reached by steps on west. Pair of late 17th century windows inserted in south wall.

WOODHEAD, Askerton NY 577739 Much altered derelict building originally 11m by 7m. No original original features remain. Probably built just after Gilsland survey of 1603 which notes John Armstrong as tenant here.

*Plans of Stonehouse, Naworth Park*

*Upper Denton: plans*

*Stonehouse, Naworth Park*

87

# GLOSSARY OF TERMS

ASHLAR - Masonry of blocks with even faces & square edges. AUMBRY - storage recess. BAILEY - defensible space enclosed by a wall or a palisade and ditch. BARBICAN - defensible court or porch in front of an entrance. BARMKIN - small walled court of modest defensive strength. BARTIZAN - A turret corbelled out at the top of a wall, often at a corner. BASTLE - Small defensible house containing single living room over a byre for cattle. BASTION - A projection rising no higher than the curtain wall. BRATTICE - A covered wooden gallery at the summit of a wall for defending its base. CORBEL - A projecting bracket supporting other stonework or timbers. CURTAIN WALL - A high enclosing stone wall around a bailey. EMBATTLED - provided with a parapet with indentations (crenellations). JAMB - A side of a doorway, window or opening. KEEP - A citadel or ultimate strongpoint. The term is not medieval and such towers were then called donjons. LIGHT - A compartment of a window. LOOP - A small opening to admit light or for the discharge or missiles. MACHICOLATION - A slot for dropping or firing missiles at assailants. MERLONS - The upstanding portions of a parapet. MOAT - A defensive ditch, water filled or dry. MOTTE - A steep sided flat-topped mound, partly or wholly man-made. PARAPET - A wall for protection at any sudden drop. PELE or PEEL - Originally a palisaded court, later coming to mean a bastle or tower house. PLINTH - The projecting base of a wall. It may be battered (sloped) or stepped. PORTCULLIS - A wooden gate made to rise and fall in vertical grooves. POSTERN - A back entrance or lesser gateway. RINGWORK - An embanked enclosure of more modest size than a bailey, generally bigger but less high than a motte summit. SHELL KEEP - A small stone walled court built upon a motte or ringwork. SOLAR - A private living room for the lord and his family. TOWER HOUSE - Self contained defensible house with the main rooms stacked vertically. WALL-WALK - A walkway on top of a wall, always protected by a parapet. WARD - A stone walled defensive enclosure. YETT - iron gate on hinges.

# PUBLIC ACCESS TO THE SITES   Codes used in the gazetteers.

E   Buildings in the care of English Heritage. Fee payable at some sites.
F   Buildings to which there is free access at any time.
H   Buildings currently used as hotels, restaurants, shops, etc.
O   Buildings opened to the public by private owners, local councils, etc.
V   Buildings closely visible from public roads, paths, churchyards & open spaces.

# FURTHER READING

Castles and Fortified Towers of Cumberland, Westmorland and Lancashire North of the Sands, J.F.Curwen 1913
Castles of Cumberland and Westmorland, R.Hugill, 1977
Castles of Cumbria, M.J.Jackson, 1990
The Old Manorial Halls of Westmorland and Cumberland, M.W.Taylor, 1892
History of Cumberland, W.Hutchinson, 2 vols 1794, reprinted 1974
History and Antiquities of Cumberland and Westmorland, Nicholson & Burn 1777
The Medieval Fortified Buildings of Cumbria, Denis R.Perriam & John Robinson, 1998
Royal Commission Historical and Ancient Monuments Inventory Westmorland, 1936
Shielings and Bastles R.C.H.A.M. 1970    Victoria County History of Lancashire
Cumberland & Westmorland - Buildings of England Series. Nikolaus Pevsner 1967
Transactions of Cumberland and Westmorland Antiquarian and Archaeological Soc.
English Heritage guides are availaible for: Brough, Brougham, Carlisle, and Lanercost
The National Trust has a guide for Sizergh Castle.
See also periodicals like: Country Life, Archeological Journal, Medieval Archeology